What's being said about BeHappy!

"After reading this magnificent book, the lessons learned in BeHappy! *are ones that I could use immediately in my own life, and which I'm confident could help anyone achieve greater happiness. The lessons are profound, yet they are simple to put into practice. Certainly, it takes time and energy to be happy, yet Jimmy has presented a winning formula that anyone can utilize in a painless manner. I highly recommend* BeHappy! *to anybody that is happy, is unhappy, or is hoping to be happy. I look forward to reading* BeHealthy! BeBalanced! BeSuccessful! *and the other intriguing books in this series."*

> —**W. Keith Schilit, Ph.D.,** Best-selling author of 5 books on entrepreneurship, including *The Entrepreneur's Guide to Preparing a Winning Business Plan and Raising Venture Capital*

The Dalai Lama was once asked why he was so happy, and he said, 'Because it makes me feel better'. You'll feel a lot better after reading Jimmy DeMesa's wonderful blueprint for creating a happy life. Be happy by learning the principles in BeHappy!

> —**Lance Secretan, Ph.D.,** Corporate Advisor, Public Speaker, Best-selling author of 14 books, including *ONE: The Art and Practice of Conscious Leadership.*

I have taught for years that happiness is not a destination; happiness is a method of travel. For those who want to learn more about traveling with more contentment and joy in their lives, Jim DeMesa offers some real gems. This book contains some very useful insights that have helped me in very practical ways and can help anyone who yearns for greater happiness. An engaging and insightful read, I highly recommend BeHappy!

> —**David Irvine,** Best-selling author *Becoming Real: Journey To Authenticity* and *Simple Living In A Complex World*

The most terrifying day in my life was my 22nd birthday — the day my manager called me to tell me that my song 'Love and Affection' had just reached NUMBER ONE on the Billboard Hot 100 Singles Chart. Surprised? So was I. I'd always told myself since I was a little boy that all I needed to solve all of my problems was being the number one star in the world. I'd found out the hard way that, for me, even the ultimate career success didn't solve my ache for happiness.

How I WISH I'd been given Dr. DeMesa's BeHappy! *that day! It would have saved me decades of frustration and futility. What I needed was exactly what this book is: an owner's manual for my own fulfillment.* BeHappy! *gives me all the tools I so desperately needed those years ago and didn't have... explained to me not only in a logical step-by-step manner that appealed to my head, but delivered as if through the voice of your best friend, which appealed to my heart. If all of the peace, adventure, and prosperity that is BEing HAPPY matters to you, I strongly recommend you save yourself the decades I endured and READ THIS BOOK now. Well done, Jimmy! Better late than never, right?*

—**Gunnar Nelson**, #1 hitmaking, multiplatinum singer/songwriter/producer/entertainer

BeHappy!

Your Guide to the
Happiest Possible Life

Other Books of Interest from DC PRESS

Books:

If It Weren't for You, We Could Get Along!

If It Weren't for the Customer, Selling Would be Easy!

The Authentic Leader: It's About PRESENCE, Not Position

Cut the CRAP…and Resolve Your Problems

Cut the CRAP and Make the Sale

Becoming Real: Journey to Authenticity

In Search of Ethics: Men and Women of Character

Who Cares: A Loving Guide for My Future Caregivers

Money Came by the House the Other Day:
A Guide to Christian Planning and Stories of Stewardship

Unleashing Excellence: The Complete Guide to Ultimate Customer Service

Go for the Green! Leadership Secrets from the Golf Course

Retain or Retrain: How to Keep the Good Ones from Leaving

Do I Stay or Do I Go? How to Make a Wise Decision About Your Relationship

Turning People On: How to Be an Encouraging Person

Raising Children One Day at a Time: A Daily Survival Guide
for Committed Parents

The One Hour Survival Guide for the Downsized:
What You Need to Know When You're Let Go

How to Compete in the War for Talent: A Guide to Hiring the Best

366 Surefire Ways to Let Your Employees Know They Count

366 MORE Surefire Ways to Let Your Employees Know They Count

52 Ways To Live Success…From the Inside Out!

Judgment of the Wolves

The Motivating Team Leader

Equal to the Task: One Family's Journey Through Premature Birth

The Forgotten Man of Christmas: Joseph's Story

The Mulling Factor: Get Your Life Back by Taking Control of Your Career

DVD's:

Attitude Modification: Motivating Yourself Against All Odds!

BeHappy!

Your Guide to the
Happiest Possible Life

Jimmy DeMesa, M.D.

PRESS

A Division of the Diogenes Consortium

SANFORD · FLORIDA

Published by DC Press
2445 River Tree Circle
Sanford, FL 32771
http://www.focusonethics.com
407-688-1156

This book was set in Adobe Minion
Cover Design and Composition by: Jeff Hand and Jimmy DeMesa

Library of Congress Catalog Number: 2006923979
        DeMesa, Jimmy
BeHappy, Your Guide to The Happiest Possible Life
        ISBN: 1-932021-20-5

First DC Press Edition
10 9 8 7 6 5 4 3 2 1
Printed in the United States of America

TO MY DAD
(1926 — 1982)

SPECIAL THANKS

WHAT YOU ARE ABOUT TO EXPERIENCE would never have been accomplished without the help and support of a great number of people. In fact, while it is somewhat cliché, it is really true that very little is ever accomplished in life without the help and support of a great team of people. So many people have contributed to this work it would be impractical to list them all. Some people don't even know how much they helped, like members of my family.

My wife and soul mate, Jill, is a tremendous supporter of everything I do, and really, nothing I accomplish would be possible without her.

And the other woman in my life, Anita, who is one of the happiest people I know, could never be a better mother, and who really taught me the very essentials of how to BeHappy! from the earliest moments in my life.

Even my father Mario, who died in 1982 when I was 24, helped prepare me to write this book through his inspiration and education — which remains with me today.

Tony Robbins, one of the world's most renowned and successful personal development coaches, has been a business partner and a huge source of inspiration and success.

David Irvine, a best-selling author, lecturer and contributor to people's lives, helped advance the process of this book toward becoming a reality.

Neil Cantor and Sanford Mahr, who invited me into their "Masterminding Group" many years ago and taught me so much about life and the power of relationships.

Fiona Fletcher and Eve Wexler in Vancouver and Jeff Hand and Jeff Dempster in Tampa who helped provide unbiased feedback on how to make this book better.

Wolfgang Richter, who provided initial editing and was a great contributor to the quality of the final work — Thanks Wolfi.

Our families in Tampa, Ocala, and Atlanta, and our many great friends in Tampa, Newport Beach, and Vancouver, who continuously play a role in my inspiration and desire to keep creating this BeHappy! book series.

To all of you, I am eternally grateful for your contribution to my happiness and to our lives… THANK YOU!

—Jimmy DeMesa, M.D.

ABOUT THE AUTHOR

 **JIMMY DEMESA** is a physician, entrepreneur, author and speaker. He is CEO of a biotechnology company and co-founder of a thriving medical education company. Jimmy has been a business partner with personal development expert Anthony Robbins, enriching the lives of healthcare professionals by helping create better teams, processes and life balance. He and his wife, Jill, live happily in Florida with their dog, Sunny — and soon, their newborn child. They spend part of their time in Vancouver, British Columbia and Newport Beach, California.

PUBLISHER'S COMMENT

HOW MANY BOOKS do you think have been published on happiness over time? If only one could get those numbers. I bet they'd be staggering. At the same time, the question could be asked, "How many books on happiness actually worked for the readers and provided anything long lasting and truly positive over a lifetime?" I can tell you one thing, this book can have significant, truly positive, long lasting influence on your life. The only obstacle to success will be you. If you're not an obstacle to your own happiness success, then you'll most likely walk away from the experience a person in more control — and happier.

I don't know about you (but I have a guess) that like most human animals on this planet, you have had your share of unhappiness. But, in all fairness, you've most likely had more happy days than not. Nevertheless, even for those of us who are happy much of the time, there is good chance that life could be made even happier — if only we knew how that was achievable.

Sure, there are exceptions — and I sincerely hope that you're not one of them. But if you are someone who can say that their life has been largely built around feelings of unhappiness, then there really is good news for you: This book offers direction and solution.

If you are open (and "open" is the key) to having someone take the lead and if you are able to take direction, the odds are in your favor. You may be just a few hundred pages from relief. Just as in the cold relief TV commercial, after the "patient" has taken the across-the-counter medication, and you hear them exclaim, "I can breathe again!"…you may find yourself exclaiming (inside your head of course), "I can be happy again!"

No fooling. If you're not at your complete wits end, if the tide hasn't completely torn down your sandcastle, and if the events of the day (week, year, lifetime) haven't completely taken the wind out of your sails, BeHappy! might prove to be the best thing you've read in a long time.

Happiness isn't something that we can put up on a scale and weigh. Or can we? I know people (and you probably do as well), due to their positive attitude and level of happiness, can actually "weigh" the impact being happy has on their lives. How so?

Well, take for example my friend, Bob, who spent fifteen years living with one of the world's most cursed illnesses — ALS. Although he knew from the start that it was a fatal disease, he and his family made plans to keep him (and them) as active and interactive as possible. When he lost his ability to speak, he didn't despair. During the waiting period, the family created a coding system that served them all until the day he died. This coding system allowed Bob to communicate with his wife and children, as well as his many friends. It also allowed him (even though completely paralyzed) to write short letters, articles, and two complete books — which I am proud to say, I published. (The technique that was devised to enable him to "write" is a story unto itself.) Bob's desire to educate people on what it was like to live with ALS, to share his opinions (for which he had thousands) with others, to manage his fantasy baseball team, and get to know his new grandchildren motivated him every day.

On a wall, placed directly in his line of sight (so he could always see it), hung a photograph of his favorite ball player — Ernie Banks of the Chicago Cubs. Banks was the consummate baseball hero. He always has a good attitude, he'd sign autographs (without charging a fee), he loved the fans, and he always played hard. Ernie is best known for a remark he made prior to a game — after hearing someone say that it was a good day to play baseball. He replied, "It's a beautiful day for a ballgame... Let's play two!" This was his way of letting everyone around him know that he would prefer playing a double-header. He had that much love for the game. That was how Bob saw life and he was always ready for "more."

Was Bob a happy person? All you had to do was ask him. He'd code you an answer as quickly as possible. There were days that he was incredibly tired and worn down by the disease. Then there days that he was upset and cranky — just like any of us. There were other days when you couldn't shut him up and he'd code for hours — until he wore out as many as three interpreters (I witnessed one such event. It's hilarious.)

Some days were really rough — such as living through the 1994 Northridge earthquake. On that day, just after the quake hit and buildings came down and people died, Bob sat in his living room, unable to move, viewing the events through eyes that were fixed straight ahead. Neighbors, concerned about the family and the possibility of gas leaks or even an explosion, got to an outside wall and made an effort to turn off the flow of gas. They didn't know that someone from the family had already gone outside and closed off the flow. The gas had been turned off, but the well-intentioned neighbors had turned it back on. Again, the family had to go back and turn the gas off. Bob immediately saw the humor in this almost comedic scene that was taking place.

On another occasion, Bob was alone in his living room, while a caregiver was working elsewhere in the house. Without warning, Bob felt himself getting dizzy. It didn't take long for him to realize that the breathing equipment that kept his lungs pumped and active, had stopped functioning. When you're unable to breathe for yourself, and in complete need of the tube in your throat to deliver that next flow of air into your lungs, it strikes me that the most of us would loose it. Not Bob.

He remained calm, knowing that losing control might be his end. As soon as the caregiver walked into the room, Bob waited for their eyes to meet. When asked if he had something to say, Bob attempted to code a message that would get the young man to check the plug in the wall (to see if it had become dislodged). As Bob later told the story, the caregiver just stared at him, unmoving. Eventually, for reasons Bob never completely understood, the caregiver seemed to get a flash. He turned toward the wall, stared at the plug, walked to the wall, and jiggled the plug. In an explosion that Bob never got over, air rushed from the machine, through the tube and filled his now deflated lungs. That event wasn't just a story of survival. How much time had elapsed isn't known for sure…but it is a fact that is lasted for minutes (not seconds). To Bob it became a humorous moment — one to always recall when future times got tough. Why not? He had survived and harder times lay ahead. He was happy that he been given more time to enjoy life (Yes — "enjoy" life).

Being happy isn't just a phrase you hear on Dr. Phil or Dr. Laura. It doesn't have to be a "sometime thing." Happiness can be a choice or the result of a series of choices. Sure, the outside world has tremendous influence on us individually, as a member of a group or team, our family — all of us. But it really is our decision as to how we'll let events impact us. If people survived the Nazi concentration camps and didn't give up on life, if the worst illnesses and disabilities don't destroy some patients' desire to overcome and go on, if family and friends of those lost on September 11, 2001 can pull themselves together and look forward to tomorrow, there must be lessons that we can all learn about happiness. If the worst of times can't destroy people, then daily events and challenges can be met head on. You can live, as Jimmy DeMesa would put it, "in freedom, not fear," and be happy more often than not.

Jimmy DeMesa is a man of wide ranging experiences and abilities. He brings them to the pages of this book and shares his own wisdom in a highly readable style. If the reader takes the time to "read" with their eyes, head and heart, there is a good chance that the happiness meter will edge up a few notches — maybe many notches. Give it a shot. You have nothing to lose and so very much to gain.

Dennis McClellan
Publisher, DC Press

PREFACE

You <u>can</u> be happier than you are today...

It's true, you really can. It's easier for some people — but not as easy for others. Circumstances can play a role. Even your "personality" (the result of your genetics and upbringing) can have an affect. However, regardless of your situation, it just takes some fundamental concepts and the ***consistent*** use of a few simple tools to achieve the happiest life possible.

> *If you are not very happy right now, this book could change your life. If you feel you are already very happy, this book can take you to a new level. Even if you just feel you could be just a bit happier, this book can help greatly.*
>
> ***Many of the people who have read this book so far have experienced a profound effect on their ability to be happier!***

Do you know someone who is always happy and upbeat? If so, think about that person. Why are they that way? Is it just the way they are — were they born that way — or is it some secret they know that others don't? These people usually have loads of friends and seem to just be "lucky" at everything.

You may also know someone who never seems to be really happy — someone who is always a bit "down", even though they appear to have everything they need for a great life. But there's just no passion or excitement in his or her life — at least not for any extended period of time.

This type of person generally complains a lot and usually can't seem to maintain solid, long lasting, fulfilling relationships.

Hopefully this doesn't describe you, but if it does (even slightly), this book could help you "come alive" and become one of those people who lives life to the fullest and who everyone loves to be around. It could change your life forever.

> *The goal of this book is to help make you happier than you are today. And, if you are already very happy, this book can invigorate that happiness in ways you may not have thought possible.*

Many psychologists believe there is a genetic component to happiness. Even if that's true, we can all **be happier** in life, regardless of our genetic predisposition or our circumstances.

This is possible regardless of your financial situation, emotional state, career status, or other personal circumstances. Like many things in life, however, it's a journey or process — not an event. And like every journey, it begins with a single step and requires a map. This book will assist you in taking that first step — providing the map, and much more.

> *"A journey of a thousand miles begins with a single step."*
> —*Confucius*

This is the first volume in a comprehensive new personal development series called BeHappy!, which can help take you to a level of fulfillment and gratitude you never imagined possible.

This book is about LIFE! Specifically, about improving it. I have created an acronym from the word 'LIFE', which is:

Living In Freedom Everyday

Many people are unfortunately
Living In Fear Everyday

Think about how much of a difference just one letter can make.

Living In Freedom Everyday
can lead to happiness

Living In Fear Everyday
can lead to unhappiness

The goal of this book is to make the change that simple.

So let's get started. Enjoy the trip. BeHappy!

CONTENTS

INTRODUCTION

HAPPINESS IS A FUNDAMENTAL NEED and desire for everyone. Regardless of our goals, financial status, level of success or current personal situation, most of what we do is — in one way or another —an attempt to make us happier.

The good news is that anyone and everyone can achieve a greater, more robust level of happiness. It's unfortunate, however, that there are so many people who are not truly happy. And for those who are happy, most want to be happier. But how?

> *"Everyday brings a chance for you to draw in a breath, kick off your shoes, and dance."*
>
> *—Oprah Winfrey*

That's the question answered in this book. The tools revealed here can help you experience whatever level of happiness you desire and commit to achieving. Even if you already consider yourself very happy, the techniques presented can help you appreciate and enjoy life more than you ever thought possible.

I recently read the book, *Nothing Is Impossible*, by Christopher Reeve. I found it to be a great read with many valuable messages. One of those messages relates to a basic appreciation for the inherent potential in every one of us to BeHappy!

As most of you know, Christopher Reeve was the actor who played Superman in the very successful movie series during the 1980's and early 1990's, and who became a quadriplegic at the age of 42, in 1995, when a horse riding accident resulted in a severe spinal cord injury.

Although I had the privilege of meeting Mr. Reeve once, I did not know him personally. Reading his words, however, made me realize that, in spite of the tremendous personal tragedy he and his family suffered, he was a happy man — all the way until his death in 2004 from a serious infection at the age of 52.

Undoubtedly he experienced anger and frustration related to his accident, and he surely must have asked himself the question, "why me?" many times. His life was obviously quite different and very difficult after the accident. But even under those terrible and challenging circumstances, it was apparent that he remained genuinely happy.

It may have been an *inward power of his soul* that enabled him to continue *appreciating* the beauty of life and the love of his family and friends. In some ways he may have even *enjoyed the process* of his "recovery," partly due to the great *relationships* he had in his life — especially his loving wife and soul mate, Dana, who stayed by him throughout all of his challenges. You will learn more about how *relationships* affect happiness, and vice versa, in Chapter Four.

As a result of the accident, Christopher Reeve created a whole new *purpose* for his life and was busier, and perhaps more fulfilled, after the accident than he was before. This concept of life's *purpose* will be addressed in Chapter Two.

Yes, anyone — literally *everyone* — can BeHappy! But depending on where you are starting and where you want to end up, like most other things in life, it takes work, effort, and commitment. And as the old saying goes, the more you put in, the more you get out.

BeHappy! is the "title track" in a new series of books intended to enhance your life and guide you to an understanding of what each of us can do to become happier — and then create an action plan to get there. By using some of the tools described in this first book, you should begin to realize an improved sense of well being that

> *"To live happily is an inward power of the soul."*
> —*Marcus Aurelius*

Are you as happy as you want? If not, why? What is it that's not letting you be as happy as possible? If so, could you be happier and what would it take to get there?

This book is intended for anyone who wants to be happier. Whether you are already very happy and just want more joy and fulfillment, or you are not very happy and need major change, this book can help.

In fact, what is happiness anyway? Could you have a totally happy life after the death of a parent? What about life after the death of a spouse or the loss of the use of your body due to an injury?

Could you ever really be happy again? The answer is yes, but depending on your circumstances, it may not be easy.

***THIS BOOK CAN HELP TO SOME DEGREE UNDER ANY CIRCUMSTANCES.** It can allow you to be happier regardless of your current situation.*

can create a foundation for you to uncover and live the most outstanding life possible.

Since happiness is a very complex and personal matter, parts of this book are not quick, easy reading. Some chapters involve thought-provoking exercises, which will help you form the basis for the *Happiness Plan* you will create at the end. But don't fret. The journey is well worth it.

As an example of how complex and broad this subject can be, even your health is an important component of the journey. But the connection may be quite different than you think. While maintaining optimal health is certainly a factor leading to greater happiness, it is my opinion as a physician that happiness itself actually leads to better health. And there is considerable growing medical evidence indicating that psychology has a major impact on disease, both positive and negative. This concept is addressed in Chapter Five — "BeHappy! *to* BeHealthy".

All this and more will be addressed as part of a remarkable and powerful journey toward total happiness. For now, it should be safe to assume you are reading this book because you want to be happier and, just as importantly, that you believe you can be happier. This attitude is critical for you to achieve a successful outcome — not just for a moment in time, but over the

---

Key Point: *The goal is to help create true, life-long happiness.*

---

long term — because the goal here is for you to achieve a true, deep, life-long sense of happiness and fulfillment.

So, I encourage you — read on, and commit to completing Part One, — (*The Foundation*) — which lays out the basic structure for happiness in your

---

IMPORTANT ADVICE:

To achieve the objective of this book and get the most out of it, it is essential that you DO the exercises by **FILLING IN** *the blanks provided.*

If you prefer not to write in the book, separate pages can be found at the back of the book in Appendix 3, with all the exercises from each chapter. These pages can be removed for future use or privacy.

---

life by providing some fundamental concepts to help you uncover what makes you happiest.

Chapter Three, entitled *What Makes You Happy?* is the most introspective part of the book, requiring considerable thought and reflection on your part. You will use your personal *Definition of Happiness*, which you will develop in Chapter One, to come to understand the basic factors related to what could make you *happiest* in the future.

In Part Two, three essential elements — *relationships*, *health*, and *money* — will be presented which can make the difference between total happiness and an unfulfilled life. Regardless of your *Definition of Happiness*, these elements can have profound effects on you.

While writing his book, I created an acronym for the word **LIFE** — *Living In Freedom Everyday*. To me, this helps create happiness. The opposite occurs by changing just one word, making it *Living In Fear Everyday*. Freedom helps create happiness; fear can destroy it. This is the kind of impact these *essential elements* can have on your life. Because great relationships, good health, and financial security allow us to live in freedom, whereas bad relationships, poor health, and money worries can cause us to consistently live in fear.

Part Three of this journey deals with *Reality*, which will help you manage some of the difficult, painful, real-world challenges we all face in life so you can BeHappy! regardless of your circumstances, and be better prepared to create your life's *Happiness Plan* in Part Four. This *Happiness Plan* will guide you, day-by-day, toward optimal happiness and fulfillment — even during the inevitable tough times we all experience in our lives.

All this will start you on an excursion toward a life of total and complete happiness. So commit to it now and embark on the journey. I look forward to having you join me on this exciting trip.

It is important to remember that this book contains many tools, opinions, and concepts which can lead to greater happiness. Like any toolbox, not every tool in the box is needed at all times. There are some tools you may rarely or never use. There are others you might not even like. That's fine. Don't use those. The philosophy is to pick the tools needed for your specific circumstances, needs, and beliefs, and use those. The others may become relevant later (or maybe not). You never know.

—**Jimmy DeMesa, MD**
2006

PART ONE

The Foundation

"Foundation" here refers to the fundamentals by which success in this program are built. Without these basic principles, true happiness will most likely not be achieved. They form the basis for everything else in the book — and in life!

This is what it will take to truly BeHappy!

1

YOUR DEFINITION
OF HAPPINESS

OBJECTIVES OF THIS CHAPTER

- To create your own personal *Definition of Happiness* (what happiness means to you) which will be the basis for achieving total happiness.

- Develop a preliminary checklist of criteria for life-long happiness.

- To understand the meaning of happiness and how true happiness is unrelated to life's difficult, painful, and challenging times.

- To begin the process of creating your life's *Happiness Plan* that will be used as a daily guide.

I WAS HAVING A CUP OF COFFEE one day with a long-time friend and business partner in Tampa, Florida. He had built a very successful real-estate development company over the past several years, working most recently with Donald Trump on one of the premier residential towers in downtown Tampa. He is a great guy, very successful, and has everything anyone could want: a wonderful family, a big, beautiful home, a new Rolls Royce, a new Bentley, a new Porsche Carrera GT, and shirts which can cost more than my entire wardrobe.

That morning as we were chatting I was thinking about how carefree and adventurous his life must be. So I asked him about his happiness. Surprisingly his reply was, *"Jimmy, I think I'm happy. But I'm not sure I really know what happiness is or what it is that would make me totally happy".*

This is a very common phenomenon. Most times, we don't know what happiness really is or what we need in our lives to make us happy. We simply keep on striving to be happy, without

> *"Many men go fishing all their lives without knowing that it is not fish they are after."*
> **—Henry David Thoreau**

really knowing what it will take. It's no wonder many people never get there.

With this reality in mind, our first step is to start the process of being completely happy the right way. And the first thing to do when embarking on any journey is to know where you are and where you want to go. It is a fundamental technique for setting and reaching any goal or destination, and our goal is to be as happy as possible.

To reach that goal, the first step is to know your outcome by defining, in detail, what happiness really means to you. This *Definition of Happiness* is completely individual — it is different for everyone — and extremely important to the process. Also, it may not be totally obvious at first.

For one person, *happiness* may relate to the achievement of a specific job, career, or social status, while for another, *happiness* may be possible only with a certain special relationship, fitness level, or financial achievement. Others may require all of these accomplishments in order to BeHappy! And finally, there might be others for which none of these are necessary for happiness. It all depends on a personal *Definition of Happiness*. And unlike the more obvious tangible goals of attaining a specific job or financial status, living a totally happy life may be a much more emotional, subjective target.

Because of these differences, as well as the concept of always "beginning with the end in mind"[1], the first step in our journey to BeHappy! is to define as specifically as possible what happiness means to you. Once you establish

this personal *Definition of Happiness*, you will be in a much better position to identify the steps required to meet that goal and create your Happiness Plan — which will be your "map" for the journey. Like a map on any major journey, this is essential to reaching your destination.

Beginning with the end in mind helps in achieving any goal. So once you are clear about what happiness means for you personally, it will be important for you to always keep that definition — the end result — in mind throughout the process. Because, once the goal is defined and that picture of the end result is visible, it will become integrated into your subconscious, making the desired result more achievable. In addition, keeping the end in mind makes it easier to adjust your plan when the landscape changes and circumstances or events take you off course. It also helps you enjoy the process and the final result much more.

Before going any further, one thing must be clearly understood. *Happiness* is a complex matter involving many emotions — mostly short-term, which will not necessarily make you a happy person. Joy, fun, contentment, and peace of mind, for example, are all positive emotions which can contribute to your happiness, but will not make you a happy person by themselves — even if they appear frequently in your daily life. These *emotions* are generally temporary, superficial feelings that can last a fleeting minute, a day, a week, a month, or even longer, but do not create fundamental happiness by themselves.

Anyone, in fact, can experience several of these emotions daily and still be unhappy overall. You may know of people who lead adventurous, fun-filled, exciting lives, but are not really happy. Some of the most visible, well known examples that come to mind are certain celebrities we often read about. While they may seem to have it all — fame, fortune, and a glamorous, exciting life — they can still be unhappy, lonely and unfulfilled. A common occurrence for some people in this situation is to turn to drugs or other distractions to fill the void in their lives.

One principle reason for this is that these people are not fulfilling their personal *Definition of Happiness*, often because they have never taken the time to thoroughly understand what would really make them happy. For these people, and for most people in general, there is much more to their true personal *Definition of Happiness* than just fame, wealth, and adventure. In fact, regardless of your *Definition of Happiness*, it is likely that fortune and fame will only go so far. Other things, such as good health, solid relationships, and a sense of contribution are also important for most of us to

BeHappy! These factors will be considered as you create your personal *Definition of Happiness*.

The converse of what was stated previously in regard to positive emotions is also true about negative emotions. Many negative feelings such as sadness, loss, boredom, and worry are generally short-term sensations that cannot make us unhappy if we are already truly happy. Having said that, if too many of these negative emotions build up over time, optimal happiness can suffer, but will not be eliminated completely if you are fulfilling your *Definition of Happiness*.

It must also be said that some negative emotions, like *regret*, can be stronger than others and therefore have the potential to jeopardize your ability to ever become totally happy. That is why there will be a focus on a few of these separately throughout the book (Chapter Nine, for example, is all about *regrets*).

As stated before, the goal of this book is to provide you with the tools necessary to assist in the production of the greatest, overall, sustainable sense of happiness possible — by creating an internal consciousness that transcends any short-term emotion or activity — even a profoundly negative one. This means that no matter what happens in your life, you will be able to stay fundamentally happy overall, even in the midst of great pain, which we all experience in life at some point. As an example, let me relay a personal story...

Throughout my life I always maintained a great relationship with both of my parents. My father was a quiet, kind, gentle man, who always wanted to become a doctor when he was growing up. But family and financial circumstances prevented him from pursuing that dream. He simply couldn't afford to go to medical school, having to work full time as a young adult to help support his family.

Consequently, when I was accepted into medical school, he was incredibly proud, beaming with joy at my achievement. It was almost as if he were going himself and he could not wait to see me achieve that which he had dreamed about for his life.

Tragically, however, during my second year in med school he died unexpectedly of a severe, untreatable pneumonia, at the very young age of 57. I was 24 at the time. One evening we were eating pizza together at a local restaurant near the school and a week later I was attending his funeral. He never saw me graduate from medical school. That week, and the subsequent months, was the worst time of my life. The pain and sadness were so intense, I wondered if I would ever be able to laugh again, much less BeHappy! If you have ever lost someone that close to you, you understand how I felt. But despite all that, even in the midst of that intense emotional pain, had I been asked the question, "are you a happy person?", I would have still been able to say 'yes' in the true sense of what, for me, being happy really means.

The point is this — even during times of intense pain or stress, our goal is to still BeHappy! overall, even if it is not recognizable at the moment. This is only achievable by creating and fulfilling your own personal *Definition of Happiness*. This is the same phenomenon which made Christopher Reeve a happy person despite having to endure some of the most painful circumstances imaginable.

> **Key Point:** *To be as happy as possible in life, your **Definition of Happiness** must be fulfilled as completely as possible.*

To achieve this deep sense of internal happiness requires a clear understanding of what happiness means to you. Therefore, the first step in this book is an interactive process designed to create your personal *Definition of Happiness*.

This is not a personal mission statement or declaration of your purpose in life. It is much more basic. It simply means answering the question: what would make you a happy person if your life included everything in your *Definition of Happiness*?

This may not be an easy question to answer, and you may want to write it first on a separate piece of paper since you may change it several times before getting it the way you want. Or you might want to start by listing a few things that could make you happier, and then use this list to construct

Children are a great source
of happiness.

your *definition*. And, there is no right or wrong *definition*. The main requirement is that your *definition* states your true feelings and includes everything required for you to be as happy as possible.

Also, I have found that it is best to not have too many or too few criteria required for your happiness. In other words, if you have only one criterion and it doesn't work out as planned, it will be difficult for you to BeHappy! For example, if your *Definition of Happiness* were simply to become wealthy, you could never BeHappy! if that didn't happen for some reason. This could be **part** of your definition, but it should not be your entire definition.

Similarly, if there are too many criteria for you to meet in your *definition*, it is difficult to get them all aligned and you will likely not achieve true happiness. Consequently, this is why I recommend you have no less than three (3) and no more than five (5) criteria.

Here are some guidelines for designing your *Definition of Happiness*:

1. At least 3 and at most 5 criteria should be included in your definition.

2. Achieving each of these criteria should be at least partially within your control.

3. At least 2 of the criteria should be relatively easy to achieve.

4. Each criterion should motivate you and give you a positive feeling.

By following these guidelines for creating your *Definition of Happiness*, you will have taken the pivotal first step toward achieving the BeHappy! goal. Take all the time you need to write your own *Definition of Happiness* here:

As you contemplate your own requirements for happiness, consider questions like:

- Is money, wealth, or the things money can buy or do important?

- Is having a purpose or contributing something to the world a factor?

- Is happiness related to your children in some way?

Is adventure important to your Definition?

- What role, if any, does personal growth play in your ability to BeHappy!?

- What role, if any, does your career play in your ability to BeHappy!?

- Are certain relationships critical to your happiness?

- What about fun, variety, adventure, or travel?

- What are your talents and are you using them?

Some thoughts about happiness I have come across in my research are:

- ❑ The supreme happiness of life is the conviction that we are loved.

- ❑ Happiness is freedom and peace of mind.

- ❑ In about the same degree as you are helpful, you will be happy.

- ❑ Happiness is living your purpose.

- ❑ Happiness requires growth, accomplishment, and success.

- ❑ Having someone to share life with creates happiness.

- ❑ Happiness is giving love, taking risks, and accepting failure.

- ❑ Living in the moment is the only way to be happy.

- ❑ Happiness is Cash Flow (actually the name of a boat in Newport Beach, CA).

- ❏ Variety, adventure, and change make up happiness.
- ❏ Happy are those who have sought and found how to serve.
- ❏ Happiness is in the doing; not in the getting.
- ❏ Success does not create happiness; happiness creates success.
- ❏ The more you accomplish, the happier you will be.
- ❏ Happiness is an ability to live your life in your own way; with great relationships, financial abundance, physical vitality, peace-of-mind, and contribution.

Your *Definition of Happiness* may or may not contain some of these concepts.[2] Most important is that it is your *Definition*. It must fit you and be meaningful to you. You should even feel some emotion when you read it, because once you have achieved a life totally consistent with **your definition**, nothing can make you unhappy, regardless of the difficulties you experience in your life. Problems and negative circumstances can and will cause you pain, stress and even sadness, but if you are fulfilling your *Definition of Happiness* completely, these effects will be temporary and will not make you an unhappy person.

> *Key Point: If you are truly happy according to your specific personal Definition of Happiness, nothing can make you unhappy — even intensely negative situations or circumstances.*

Just as negative circumstances cannot make you an unhappy person if you are fulfilling your *Definition of Happiness*, positive events or circumstances cannot make you a happy person if you are not fulfilling the elements of that personal *definition*. So again, crafting this *Definition of Happiness* is a very important first step.

For example, in 2005, cyclist and cancer survivor Lance Armstrong won the prestigious *Tour de France* for the seventh consecutive year; becoming the first person in history to achieve this incredible feat.[3] As he stepped up to the podium to receive the glorious recognition for his victory, he surely must have experienced many positive emotions. So does that make him a happy person? The answer is yes only if three requirements are met: (1) this achievement somehow helped fulfill part of his *Definition of Happiness*, (2) at least part of the "essential elements" (discussed in Part Two) are a positive part of his life and (3) the other criteria in his definition are also being fulfilled. All three are important.

Lance Armstrong after winning the *Tour de France.*

The previous point about short-term emotions is at play here. As euphoric as his achievement made him feel at the moment, fulfillment of all the criteria in his *Definition of Happiness* are essential for true sustainable happiness.

In other words, Lance Armstrong's *Definition of Happiness* is probably NOT, "to win seven consecutive *Tour de France* competitions." It may not even include anything specifically about his success in cycling. Undoubtedly this athletic aspect of his life probably represents a very significant, positive, and happy moment for him and may contribute greatly to achieving his overall *Definition of Happiness*; but it will certainly not result in lifelong happiness by itself. In time, the emotion from this event will fade and other, more significant factors related to true happiness must be involved.

If you've read Lance Armstrong's books, *It's Not About the Bike* and *Every Second Counts*, you can see that his *Definition of Happiness* relates as much or more to family and contribution than to fame, wealth or bike racing. If Lance Armstrong were to write his *Definition of Happiness*, it might be something like this:

> *I will be happy if I am living life to the fullest with my children, a woman I love, and great adventure, while doing my best at everything I do, and contributing all I can to those going through the pain and suffering of cancer.*

This hypothetical *Definition of Happiness* for Lance Armstrong includes five criteria for his happiness — (1) spending time with his children, (2) having a great relationship with a woman he loves, (3) being the best at what he does, (4) living life to the fullest with great adventure, and (5) contributing to those fighting cancer. If he fulfills each of these criteria in his life, he will **BeHappy!** whether he wins the *Tour de France* or not.

As you can see by the hypothetical definition above, it includes:

1. Five criteria (within the 3-5 criteria guideline).

2. They are all at least partially within his control.

3. Two are *relatively* easy to achieve (e.g., time with his children).

4. All certainly motivate him and give him positive fulfillment.

Assuming the above *Definition of Happiness* accurately represents Lance Armstrong's views, winning the *Tour de France* can contribute to his overall happiness since it provides evidence of being the best. But if he were not living life to the fullest or spending time with his children or helping people with cancer, I suspect his life would be somewhat empty overall and he would not be as happy.

Think about it. If Lance Armstrong were to win the *Tour de France* every year, but was never able to see his children, find love in his life or help people with cancer, do you think he would really **BeHappy!**? Read his books and I'm sure you will agree the answer is *no* — as well as being inspired by his story.

Contrasting this *Definition of Happiness* concept with a personal mission statement is important. Your *Definition of Happiness* relates more to **how you live** or **what you need** in your life to **BeHappy!** (it is about you) whereas a personal mission statement (which relates to your purpose in life) is linked more to **what you will contribute to the world and others**. Both are important, but for this first step in the **BeHappy!** journey, it is important to define what you **need** in your life to be happiest.

To illustrate the difference between your *Definition of Happiness* and a *personal mission statement*, re-read my concept of Lance Armstrong's version as stated earlier and you will see it relates to what he needs in his life to be happiest. In contrast, if I were to write my hypothetical concept of Lance Armstrong's personal *mission statement*, it might be:

> *To help cancer patients around the world by being an example of possibility, strength, and inspiration — both physically and mentally.*

Hopefully you can see how this hypothetical *personal mission statement* differs from the previous *Definition of Happiness*. The mission statement is focused on what he can *contribute* (i.e., focused on what others need). It is what motivates him. It helps fulfill his sense of contribution, but it is only a small piece of what he needs to be totally happy in life.

Key Point: *The fewer criteria you require for happiness, the easier it will be to achieve the happiest life possible.*

The degree to which you can **BeHappy!** is directly related to the degree to which you fulfill your *Definition of Happiness*. That's why it is so important to start considering what it will take to make you happy. So make sure to work on it seriously. In fact, you should not proceed into the next chapter until you have it the way you want it, even if it takes a few days to think about and fine-tune. True happiness is worth the time.

Also, make sure it is not a mission statement, but rather a true representation of what you need in your life to **BeHappy!** Make sure it is as complete and accurate as possible **under today's circumstances**. Use the guidelines on page 6. This is an iterative process and you can revise it as needed later because your definition can change over time. In fact, Lance Armstrong's definition surely changed significantly after his difficult battle with cancer. Before the cancer experience there was probably nothing in his *definition* about helping cancer patients. But afterwards, he had a new *purpose* in his life (a new mission) that now adds to his personal happiness if he is satisfying it (and probably reduces his happiness if he is not satisfying it).

To finish this chapter, write the 3-5 main criteria from your *Definition of Happiness* in the space below or in Appendix 3. You should refer back to this list frequently as a checklist or reminder for the fulfillment of your *definition*.

My Criteria for Happiness:

-
-
-
-
-

CHAPTER SUMMARY & KEY POINTS

1. Your *Definition of Happiness* is your destination on this journey.

2. A person's *Definition of Happiness* is very individual and must be fulfilled completely to be optimally happy in life.

3. Your *Definition of Happiness* is not a personal mission statement or declaration of your purpose in life.

4. If you are fulfilling your *Definition of Happiness* completely, nothing can make you unhappy over the long-term.

5. Think about what you need in your life to be happy. If you now know better than before, you are further ahead than most people.

2

IDENTITY, PURPOSE, AND PASSIONS

OBJECTIVES OF THIS CHAPTER

- To understand how living consistent with your identity is critical to happiness.
- To clarify how your purpose in life determines your happiness.
- Identifying your passions (what you love) and how they can help you to be happier.
- Learning the 4 Key Questions you can use to BeYou!

HAVING ESTABLISHED YOUR DESTINATION in Chapter One by creating your personal *Definition of Happiness*, the goal of this chapter is to address three fundamental factors that influence happiness greatly. This will lead to the exercises in Chapter Three which, when combined with these fundamentals, will determine the starting point of your journey. Once you have a clear view of these two points — the start and the finish — you can begin to create your map or plan to get to that destination of true happiness.

The three fundamental factors are your *identity*, your *purpose* and your *passions*. This chapter will help you start using these to uncover their impact on your life and direct you on how they can best be employed to make you happier.

It is important to first consider the relative correlation between your *identity*, *purpose* and *passions*, and the degree to which they can influence happiness. That relationship can be represented by this simple pie chart[4]:

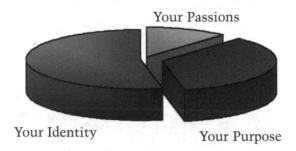

Your Passions

Your Identity   Your Purpose

As you can see from this chart, I feel your *identity* has the most impact on happiness — contributing about 60-70% of your abiltity to **BeHappy!** on a relative basis. Your *identity* refers to knowing *who you are* as a person and living in harmony with that *identity*.

Next in importance, after your *identity*, is your *purpose*. This refers to *why you are here* or what you can *contribute* to the world to **BeHappy!** This makes up between 15% and 25% of the effect on your happiness.

Finally, the third important factor relates to your passions or what you *love to do*, which makes up about 5-15% of what it takes to **BeHappy!**

> **Key Point:** *Living consistent with your identity (who you really are) is more important to happiness than having a purpose or having a career involving something you are passionate about.*

The relative influence these three factors have on happiness explains why it is more critical to live consistent with our *identity* to **BeHappy!** than it is to have a job or career we are completely passionate about (as described later in this chapter).

While a career involving your *passions* can surely have a positive effect, it makes up less than 15% of the requirement for happiness and, therefore, doing something consistent with your identity is much more important. In fact, living contradictory to *who you are* will lead to significant stress and unhappiness.

Having said that, the three components overlap quite a bit. In other words, defining your *identity* relates to your *purpose* and *passions* at some level and all three should be addressed to be as happy as possible. We will start with the most important — your *identity*.

YOUR IDENTITY — WHO YOU ARE

Knowing what happiness means to you, as defined in Chapter One, will form the foundation of your ultimate *Happiness Plan*. A key component of that plan requires an understanding of who you really are (i.e., your personal *identity*) and then making sure you live consistent with that *identity*.

It means going through life as the *real* you. Whether it's in a professional capacity (such as your job or career) or a personal capacity (such as raising a child), knowing who you are and living your life accordingly is essential to optimal happiness.

If applied correctly, combining a clear understanding of your *identity* with some of the tools recommended in this book should give you a great sense of joy, fulfillment, and peace of mind. This is possible since you can truly BeHappy! if you are living in sync with who you are as a person. The converse is also true: you will be unhappy, at least to some extent, if you are not living in sync with that *identity*.

In his book, *The Saint, The Surfer, & The CEO*, Robin Sharma describes an "Integrity Gap," which is basically the difference between who you really are inside, and how you act, what you do, and how you appear to others outside. According to Sharma, the greater the gap, the less happiness you will experience. The reason is, psychologically, people are only truly happy if they are living in sync with their personal "internal" *identity*.

> "*The biggest personal defeat suffered by human beings is constituted by the difference between what one was capable of becoming and what one has in fact become.*"
>
> —*Ashley Montague*

It is outside the scope of this book to delve deeper into the complex psychology associated with this concept, but it is important to identify and use as part of the process. David Irvine, another best-selling author, wrote an excellent book called *Becoming Real*, which provides great insight toward understanding your *identity* and living consistent with it.

Later in this chapter we will explore some specific aspects of your *identity* and how you can use them to **BeHappy!**

YOUR PURPOSE — WHY YOU ARE HERE

Determining your *purpose* in life (i.e., why you are here) is another factor which can influence happiness greatly. Many "self-help" programs suggest that we are all here for a reason, even if we don't yet know that reason.

Whether that is true or not, I don't know. More relevant for the goal of this book, however, is simply an understanding that "having a *purpose*" relates mostly to *contribution*. And, even if you do not know your *purpose*, you can create one in the form of a personal mission statement.

Your *purpose* could be as grandiose as leading a nation to freedom — similar to William Wallace as depicted by Mel Gibson in the movie ***Braveheart*** — or as personal as raising a child to become a productive contributor to society.

Have you ever considered whether you have a *purpose* in life? Why are you here on this planet at this point in time? What are you meant to do or *contribute* during your life? These are all questions you should answer for yourself and then use as part of your map on life's road to happiness.

> *"I'm not living the life I thought I would lead… but it does have meaning and purpose."*
> **—Christopher Reeve**

Some people know exactly why they are here. They have a compelling mission and are focused on fulfilling it. Christopher Reeve and Lance Armstrong discovered their *purpose* after personal tragedy, which motivated them and created fulfillment in their lives. Some people have never considered their *purpose*. Others place little importance on whether they have a *purpose* or not, and yet others believe they have no *purpose*. Each of these types of people can **BeHappy!** Which is it for you?

As a starting point, check the box that relates most closely to you:

❑ I know my *purpose* in life.

❑ I believe I have a *purpose* in life but do not yet know it.

❑ I believe I have no *purpose* or having a *purpose* is not impor-
tant to me.

> *Key Point: Your PURPOSE is different from the DEFINTION OF HAPPINESS you created in Chapter One. A purpose is WHY YOU ARE HERE (i.e., what you can contribute), while your DEFINTION OF HAPPINESS relates to what **you need** in your life to BeHappy! That definition may include living consistently with your purpose.*

If you checked the first box above, write down your *purpose* in the space below, just so you have it written out. Like your *Definition of Happiness* in Chapter One, if you generally know your *purpose* but have never considered it seriously, this could take some thought and time. Spend whatever time is necessary to complete it.

My *purpose* in life is:

Purpose has varying degrees of importance to each of us. And again, as the pie chart at the beginning of the chapter shows, I believe it is a smaller piece of the entire pie compared to the importance your *identity* plays. So it is not critical to define your *purpose* — or even have one — to **BeHappy!** But it can surely help. In contrast to living consistent with your *identity*, you can be quite happy without a well-defined *purpose*. You can be even happier if you know your *purpose* and are living your life in pursuit of fulfillment of that mission.

If you checked the second box (you believe you have a *purpose*, but just don't yet know it) you should explore other ways to identify and define your purpose, such as Anthony Robbins' program called *Date With Destiny*, David Irvine's book, *Becoming Real*, or Rick Warren's book, *The Purpose-Driven Life*. Soon you will also be able to refer to another book in my BeHappy! series called BeYou!, which will contain guidelines for identifying and defining your special *purpose* or personal mission.

> *"My life has no purpose, no direction, no aim, and no meaning, and yet I'm happy. I can't figure it out. What am I doing right?"*
>
> —*Charles M. Schulz*
> *(creator of "Peanuts")*

If you checked the third box and believe you have no purpose, you can still BeHappy! in the long term — especially if having a *purpose* is not important to you — by simply living true to your basic *identity* as just described. This is achievable since, referring back to the pie chart, you can see that *purpose* is a smaller piece of what is required to BeHappy! (15-25%) compared to your *identity* (60-70%). Having a *purpose* inspires *contribution*, however, so it definitely helps foster happiness by bringing more fulfillment to your life. But there are many ways to *contribute* without having a defined or specific *purpose*. This will be discussed further later.

I urge you to open your mind to the possibility that you may actually have a *purpose* in life and explore this possibility further — especially if not having a purpose causes conflict within you or leaves some emptiness in your life. There is a lot you can do to find your *purpose* — or **a** *purpose* — if you are willing to make the commitment. If *purpose* is not important to you, just being consistent with your *identity* will lead to greater happiness, especially if you are doing things you love to do (i.e., fulfilling your passions). Also, finding ways to contribute, even small ways, fills an emotional need which will make you happier.

YOUR PASSIONS — WHAT YOU LOVE TO DO

What do you love to do? What is it you could do all the time and never get tired of doing?

Is it playing music, gardening, biking, hiking, skiing, traveling, or acting? Is it reading, playing golf, or fixing up old cars? Whatever your answer to this question, it is another path on your journey toward happiness. As you saw in the pie chart at the beginning of this chapter it is not the most important, but it can add tremendously to your life.

Many personal development experts say that your job or career must relate directly to your passions to be successful and happy. I do not believe this to be completely true. Like most people, if you must work for a living — while it is unlikely you can hate your job and be totally happy in life — it really boils down to an ability to *love what you do*, rather than *do what you love*, that leads to success and happiness.

If your passion is golf or music, for example, it is not essential for you to become a professional golfer or musician to be completely happy in your life. You can surely be a pharmacist, a sales person, or an options trader and still be very happy by (a) learning to love what you do and (b) including golf or music , for eaxample, it is in other parts of your life. This will be further addressed through the creation of your *Happiness Plan* in Chapter Eleven.

Most importantly, it is critical to choose a career that is consistent with who you are as a person — your *identity* — to be truly happy. For example, if you are a person whose highest values include relationships and connecting with people, you probably would not be happiest in a job that is void of human interaction. Similarly, if you are an "outdoors person", you might not be happiest at a job that confined you to an office all day, every day. In reality, therefore, even if you were doing something you didn't absolutely love, as long as it is consistent with your *identity*, you can BeHappy!

A good example of this important principle is a sales person who does not believe in the product or service he or she is selling. It just can't last. Regardless of how great the financial rewards may be, an inner struggle will eventually get in the way if the person knows who they are and is true to themselves. Internal tension will build until a breaking point occurs and a change must be made. Even some positive aspects of the job, like a great salary, will be insufficient to fill the void in the long run. And, if a change is not made, this person will be quite troubled and never truly happy.

On the other hand, if this sales person is selling something he or she believes in (i.e., it is congruent with their *identity*), they can BeHappy! and fulfilled, even if a sales job is not something they absolutely love or the financial rewards are not outstanding.

The best scenario, of course, is for all to exist simultaneously. If you can find a job or career that is consistent with your *identity*, involves one of your true *passions* in life, and provides significant wealth-building potential, you are very fortunate — and perhaps you can be very happy. However, this is not a requirement. YOU CAN BeHappy! even if you are working at a job which does not involve one of your *passions* (as long as it doesn't make you miserable).

The opposite is also true. You can have a great career doing something you are totally passionate about and still not BeHappy! in your life overall. This again relates to that important *Definition of Happiness* from Chapter One. It also supports the hypothesis of the relatively smaller role passions play in the general scheme of things.

Again, some celebrities come to mind since they tend to live very visible lives. Surely you have heard of actors, musicians, or athletes who absolutely love what they do, living "the perfect life" with a total passion for their job, but are still unbalanced, unfulfilled and unhappy. Some turn to alcohol, drugs, or even suicide for "relief". How is this possible? It's probably because they may be living inconsistent with their true *identity* or are neglecting several parts of their *Definition of Happiness* — perhaps without even knowing it. Also, *relationships* (Chapter Four), rules (Chapter Seven), and *regrets* (Chapter Nine) could be important factors in their failure to be totally happy.

There are also some people so driven and passionate about their work that the rest of their lives are a mess. Their life is unbalanced and they often neglect their family and friends, even their health, because of their *passion* for their job. Ultimately, these people (sometimes called workaholics) are not happy since *balance* is another important component of happiness and true success in life. They also tend to eventually *regret* their intense focus on work, many times only after it's too late.

LEARNING TO LOVE WHAT YOU DO

Even if you are not passionate about your job or career, you can BeHappy! by learning to *love what you do*.

> *"It is not in doing what you like, but in liking what you do that is the secret of happiness."*
> **— James M. Barrie**

There are many ways to accomplish this. For example, if you commit to something, and become great at it, you will derive more enjoyment from it because of the self-confidence it builds, the pride it instills and the growth it represents.

The book, *First Break All the Rules* by Marcus Buckingham and Curt Coffman contains a great example of this in a story about a woman who is a data entry clerk. Exciting right? I would bet this woman probably did not consider this job something she was passionate about. Surely it was just a job — something to allow her to make a living.

According to Buckingham and Coffman, this woman set a goal of becoming the best keypunch operator ever. The national average number of data entry keypunches in a month is approximately 380,000. So, it is safe to assume some people do significantly more (perhaps double that amount for the best ones) and some quite a bit less. The average, though, is 380,000 key-punches per month. This woman got so good at her task that she began doing 560,000/month — eventually increasing to over 100,000/**day** (which is 2,000,000 per month based on a 20-day work month).

In fact, this woman gained so much speed she eventually was able to achieve 3,500,000/month, basically TEN TIMES the national average, main-taining high quality results in the process. It became something she loved doing because it was a challenge and source of pride for her. It built her self-confidence and self-esteem, eventually allowing her to teach others how to do the job better and get many professional opportunities, including a promotion, where she made more money than she ever thought possible as a consequence of her achievements. It changed her life completely.

So as you can see, by finding a way to *love what you do* (in this example it was by becoming the best at a relatively mundane job) you can be just as happy as if you are making a living doing something you already love. This not only has a direct benefit on your life, it can have many indirect benefits as well. The keypunch operator got a direct benefit by becoming the best at what she did, making her "a star" and allowing her to enjoy it much more than she thought possible. But it didn't stop there. She also got the indirect benefit of a promotion — becoming a teacher and leader. This surely provided many emotional benefits too, like pride and self esteem, as well as the likely financial benefits; giving her a new level of wealth she never thought possible, which helped improve other areas of her life. It can become a self-perpetuating growth and happiness cycle, constantly increasing the quality of life.

This can happen to you also. Even if you are in a job you don't really love, you can do one of two things. First, you could change jobs or careers, which is what I did.

For me, even though I thought becoming a doctor was my *purpose* in life — and also my passion for as long as I can remember — once I was doing it, I found many things were missing for me (my *Definition of Happiness* was not being fulfilled completely). So I went back to school, got my Masters in Business Administration and entered the business world, using my medical background as a basis. And I am much happier for it.

If you feel you cannot either change your career (although everyone can if the commitment is there) or you don't want to go through the effort and/or risk of changing careers (which is more likely the case), the second thing you can do is take ownership of the situation. Do whatever you must in order to become the best at what it is you do (like the "key punch operator" in the example above or the "bricklayer" in the example on the next page). Neither is easy, but both are worth the effort if you want to be as happy as possible.

Another Way to Love What You Do...
TAKING OWNERSHIP...

There is a great story about a construction company executive who came down to a construction site anonymously one Friday afternoon to check on some of the workers. He went up to the first of three bricklayers, a guy who seemed to be very "down" and frustrated and asked him what he was doing. The bricklayer looked at him somewhat bothered and said sarcastically, "I'm laying these bricks — what does it look like I'm doing? It's Friday afternoon and I'm just counting the hours until it's time to go home."

With that, the executive went to a second bricklayer — a guy who seemed to be in slightly better spirits — and asked him what he was doing. This bricklayer said, "I'm building this wall. I can probably finish it in another week, then move on to the next project. Right now, I'm looking forward to a great weekend."

Finally, the executive walked over to a third bricklayer, a cheerful man who was singing as he worked. Again the executive asked what he was doing, to which the "bricklayer" replied, "I am building this beautiful cathedral. It's going to be the most beautiful cathedral anyone has ever seen. Thousands of people will come here every year and I will be responsible for their ability to enjoy such a beautiful place."

*What's the difference between these three "bricklayers"? The difference is **ownership** and the pride that comes from taking ownership in what you do. The first guy was just laying bricks and he was miserable. The third guy — although doing the same activity — "owned" his job, was building something beautiful, and was happy doing it. In fact, he would probably not even call himself a bricklayer, but rather a builder. He is not laying bricks but building things that enhance people's lives.*

You can learn to love what you do by taking ownership and becoming great at what you do, whatever it is.

It is also important to know your *passions* and find a way to include as many as possible into your life outside your job or career.

UNDERSTANDING YOUR IDENTITY FOR GREATER HAPPINESS

Having established that living consistent with your *identity* is one of the most important initial criteria for happiness, you must now refine the definition of your *identity* and take the action necessary to live most congruently with that "you" (i.e., closing the gap).

In exploring this issue, there are four key questions to ask yourself in defining the real you. First: What is most important to you in life? The answer to this question establishes your values, which is essential in helping define your *identity*. And, living consistent with your values creates greater happiness. The converse is even more important since living inconsistent with your values is extremely unfulfilling and stressful.

As an example, my wife values family very highly. Because of my career, we have been living several thousand miles away from our families. Believe me, this creates discomfort, some frustration and a large phone bill — something many of you will relate to.

The second question to ask yourself as you search for the real "you" is: What roles do you play in your life? The third is: What are your standards? And the fourth is: What do you love to do? (We will build more on this last question in Chapter Three — *What Makes You Happy?*)

These questions can be very difficult to answer, but the deeper you probe and the more thoroughly you answer them, the more helpful they will be in making you happier.

So, starting with values, answer the first question: What is most important to you in life? Is health most important? Is it having chil-

> *The Key Questions for Being You:*
>
> *1. What is most important to you?*
>
> *2. What roles do you play?*
>
> *3. What are your standards?*
>
> *4. What do you love to do?*

dren or making sure your children get the best education possible? What about the rest of your family or friends? Is contribution most important? What about freedom? There are no wrong answers, so list the 3 to 5 things that are most important to you in life:

-

-

-

-

-

This list can start to define your values, which will add to the identification or affirmation of your *identity*. A concise list of your top 3-5 values can be fine-tuned later. For now, however, if you took this question seriously you should have written down the 3-5 things that are most important to you in life. In general, this is what you value most, which can help you live your life true to who you **really** are (and ultimately with what you want). We'll address **how** later.

But first, after beginning to define your values, we need to identify the major roles you play in life — what is it you do and how do you view yourself? Think about it as if you were an actor in a play — the play of life. What are the roles or parts you play in this performance? Some examples of various roles people play in life are listed in the

ROLES PEOPLE PLAY:

- ❏ *A mother or father*
- ❏ *A friend*
- ❏ *A brother or sister*
- ❏ *An artist*
- ❏ *A teacher*
- ❏ *A mentor*
- ❏ *An adventurer*
- ❏ *A contributor*
- ❏ *A doctor or lawyer*
- ❏ *An organizer*
- ❏ *A builder*
- ❏ *An entertainer*
- ❏ *An athlete*
- ❏ *A volunteer*
- ❏ *A spouse*
- ❏ *A lover*
- ❏ *A leader*
- ❏ *A manager*
- ❏ *An employee*
- ❏ *An entrepreneur*
- ❏ *A politician*
- ❏ *A writer*
- ❏ *An stock trader*
- ❏ *An investor*
- ❏ *An executive*
- ❏ *A home maker*
- ❏ *A cook*
- ❏ *A business owner*
- ❏ *An engineer*
- ❏ *A speaker*

box to the right. Consider using these as a guide to identify your major roles. Put a check in any box on the previous page that applies to you. You may be able to list many different roles. For our purposes, the 5 most important are the only ones you need to list.

List those top 5 here:

1.

2.

3.

4.

5.

This is important since, as I mentioned before, we can only BeHappy! if we are living in accord with who we are. So if you are playing roles that don't fit, you cannot BeHappy! and changes need to be made. On the other hand, if you are not playing a role that really represents who you are, it is important to somehow add this role to your life.

For example, some people see one of their roles in life as that of a parent. If they don't have children, therefore, there is likely some internal conflict and emptiness in their life. This will hinder happiness if not identified and addressed in some way.

Having listed up to 5 of your highest values (that which is most important to you in life) and up to 5 major roles you play in your life (which can represent, at least partially, your *identity*), the next step is to define your standards.

What standards do you live by on a daily basis? In other words, what are the minimum acceptable guidelines you follow, consciously or subconsciously, in dealing the world around you, and the minimum behavior you will tolerate from people with whom you interact? If you are not living up to these standards, you will not be able to achieve total happiness.

In his 4-day, intensive program, *Date With Destiny*, Tony Robbins helps people develop a "Code of Conduct", which is essentially a list of standards that describes how to commit to conducting yourself on a daily basis. Part of Tony's goal in *Date With Destiny* is to raise your standards by developing this Code and making sure you do something everyday which addresses each of the items in your own personal *Code of Conduct*. We won't get into all of that here, but we will attempt to establish your current standards as a means to clarify how you can be living in harmony with that list of standards.

To do this, answer these questions: How will you "be" in your life? What standards must you "be" true to? Here is a list of examples:

I will ...

Be honest	**Be open**	**Be strong**
Be fun	**Be passionate**	**Be loving**
Be a leader	**Be creative**	**Be nice**
Be sexy	**Be confident**	**Be adventurous**

Now write the *TOP 5* guidelines for how you must live your life (your standards):

Be

Be

Be

Be

Bc

These are your highest standards. If you follow them daily, you will be happier. It's really that simple.

Lastly, to answer the fourth question: What is it you love to do? Consider activities that, just by thinking of them, put a smile on your face or give you a good feeling inside. Consider also the talents you have (another tool for happiness if you are using those talents in your life somehow). This could be what you are passionate about in your life. Write down at least one and as many as three:

What you love to do:

Your talents (what you're really good at):

The fundamental concept to enhancing your ability to BeHappy! is to make sure the items on this list play some role in your life. For me, it's writing, music and photography. These are my passions. If I felt these activities could help me achieve everything in my *Definition of Happiness*, I would be involved in one or more as a career. In fact, I have been both a professional musician and professional photographer. They were exciting careers, but were not getting me where I wanted to be for the long-term (i.e., they did not fulfill my entire *Definition of Happiness*).

So photography and music remain positive sources of happiness and inspiration for me as hobbies. And as I mentioned, with my chosen career, I have learned to love what I do. In fact, another of my passions is travel and my current career supplies plenty of it. It helps further the love of my job. Importantly, I also have a long-term plan (part of my *Happiness Plan*) to become more seriously involved in photography, music, and writing later in my life. It's a goal for me and the reason this book, and the entire series, became possible.

So you have now answered the four basic questions used to determine who you really are (your *identity*). You know (a) what is most important to you, (b) the main roles you play (or should play) in your life, (c) the primary standards you must live by, and (d) your talents and what you love to do. With this information now clearer, you might even start to have a better sense of your *purpose* in life if you didn't know before. If you didn't write your *purpose* at the beginning of this chapter, try again here with the insights you may have gained through this exercise (and if you did write it down before, write it again here to make sure it hasn't changed since you answered these questions):

If you are still somewhat uncertain of your *purpose*, it is something you should work on as part of your journey toward total and complete happiness. We will not attempt to go any further with it here. Since it makes up about 15-25% of the fundamentals for happiness, it is clearly a factor. With the information you have from this book you should be equipped to begin figuring it out enough to get the benefits required for this part of your "life enhancement" process.

> *Key Point: Having a purpose in life provides a compelling way to contribute something to the world, however small or large. Depending on your views, it could make up about 25% of what it takes to be as happy as possible.*

Here's one idea: look over the roles you wrote for yourself earlier. If you can pick one that excites you most, or has the deepest meaning for you — then that role may be closely related to your *purpose*. For example, your role list might include, "I am a photographer." And, if reading this gives you an emotional response (such as pride, joy, confidence, or excitement), then perhaps your *purpose* in life is to contribute beauty to the world or to create memorable moments for people (to help them be happier and more fulfilled). As stated before, generally purpose relates to *contribution*.

While all this may appear somewhat simplistic, it's enough for now. It is essential that you know what is most important to you, the roles you play in your life, the standards you live by, and what you love to do.

This information will help define you and make a big difference in the degree to which you will BeHappy! You will use this information to create your *Happiness Plan* at the end of the book.

CHAPTER SUMMARY & KEY POINTS

1. Living consistent with your identity (who you really are) is one of the most critical factors affecting happiness.

2. To explore your true identity, you need to know what is most important to you in life, what roles you want to play, the standards by which you live your life, what you love to do, and what you are really good at.

3. Knowing your purpose in life and fulfilling your passions, although not as important as living consistent with your identity, can augment your happiness greatly.

3

WHAT MAKES YOU HAPPY?

OBJECTIVES OF THIS CHAPTER

- To determine what is missing from your life right now and start to understand how to add these things to your life.

- To reflect on what has made you happy throughout your life.

- To better understand what could make you happier for the rest of your life.

NOTE to Readers: *This may be the most challenging chapter in the book. It requires thought and reflection and will probably take some time to complete. Stick with it and it will pay off.*

KNOWING WHERE YOU ARE STARTING

In Chapter One, you created your personal *Definition of Happiness*. This is your ultimate destination. It represents the final result you wish to achieve, so throughout the journey this end should always be kept in mind.

In Chapter Two you discovered some foundational concepts necessary to help you complete this journey — your *identity*, your *purpose*, and your *passions* — and how to use these to be happier. These are some of the "supplies" needed for the journey, just like a car and fuel are needed for a road trip. They also help you better understand where you are today (your starting point).

The goal of this chapter is to more fully define that starting point as a way to better prepare for the design of your *Happiness Plan* partly by understanding what is keeping you from being completely happy today. This can be determined by answering two basic questions: (1) What do you feel is missing from your life? (2) What do you think could make you happier?

Although some of the answers to the first question might be the same as some of the answers to the second question, there may be some key differences. Most importantly, answering these two questions will help shed some light on the basic components of the plan you will develop later to become as happy as possible in life.

First, consider the most important things you feel may be missing from your life (if there are any). List them here:

•

•

•

Some examples are:

❑ Self-esteem	❑ Great sex	❑ A great job
❑ Playfulness	❑ Passion	❑ Excitement
❑ Time with family	❑ Adventure/Variety	❑ A soul mate
❑ Money	❑ Connection	❑ Purpose
❑ A best friend	❑ Children	❑ Fun

If you cannot think of anything significant missing from your life, you are further ahead than most people. This can help accelerate your progress. But you may still not be as happy as possible, especially if your *Definition of Happiness* is not being fulfilled completely. In fact, part of the answer to this question could be within that *definition*.

If, however, you did list anything missing from your life, depending on the magnitude, it could be affecting your happiness in some way — perhaps significantly. In either case, by using the tools in this book, you have the potential to change things very dramatically.

In this chapter we need to get very specific in identifying what you feel could make you happier. Just filling any voids listed above should make you happier. But it may not be that simple. There may be many more ways to feel happier than there are things missing from your life. For example, you may feel the only thing really missing from your life is a close, intimate relationship. Filling that void will surely make you much happier, as you will see in Chapter Four (*Relationships: The Ultimate Happiness Loop*). At the same time, you may feel more money, a better job, less stress, a more active sex life, or going back to school could augment your life and make you happier as well; even though they are not things you feel are actually missing. Remember, to be as happy as possible everything in your *Definition of Happiness* must be fulfilled.

So, it is now important to get very specific. What could be added to your life to make you happier? In the space below, write down the first 3 or 4 things that come to your mind. Use your *Definition of Happiness* from Chapter One and the list from the previous page of things missing from your life as guides (remember, some of these could be the same as in your "missing" list).

Some examples are:

- ❑ A great, passionate relationship
- ❑ Financial independence
- ❑ Having children
- ❑ Contributing more
- ❑ A new career
- ❑ Having a purpose
- ❑ Learning a new skill or craft
- ❑ Going back to school
- ❑ Becoming famous
- ❑ Traveling more
- ❑ Volunteering
- ❑ More free time
- ❑ A better job
- ❑ Less stress

As you can see from this list of examples, these can be — and should be — more specific than the general *Definition of Happiness* you developed in Chapter One.

These two lists — what is missing from your life and what could make you happier — will be used later to develop your *Happiness Plan*.

REMEMBERING WHAT HAS MADE YOU HAPPY IN YOUR LIFE

Next, it is important to get from where you are today to where you want to be in the future. This requires that you know what has already created happiness and unhappiness for you at various points throughout your life. This will be an 8-Step process that once completed will help create your "map." Let me caution you — this is the most tedious part of the book — but it is important to your ultimate happiness. Most people find this to be very enlightening and once you get through these 8 Steps, the rest of the journey is simpler and the rest of the book is much easier reading.

> **Key Point:** *This 8-step process will help solidify the foundation through which you can then use the remainder of the tools in the book to create your Happiness Plan. Take the time to complete it and the rest will be much easier.*

STEP ONE: THE PAST WEEK

In determining what has created happiness and unhappiness for you in your life, the first step involves recalling everything you have experienced **during the past week** that contributed (or could contribute) to your happiness. In other words, what was fun, fulfilling, pleasurable, or exciting for you during the past week? In the spaces below and on the next page, list everything you would consider to have been positive events, circumstances, or situations, focusing only on the past week for right now.

It is best to start with today (if it's late enough in the day) and fill in the corrsponding space provided below, since this is freshest in your memory. If it is early in the day, start with yesterday. Then work backwards until you have responded to each day for the past week. Go ahead — do it now. Think back over the past week. What was great about it?

Monday:

Tuesday:

Wednesday:

Thursday:

Friday:

Saturday:

Sunday:

Don't worry if some days are blank. If they are **all** blank, this could be an issue, but we are just getting started. To assist in thinking what you might include on the list, here is my list for the past week:

Monday: Cruised with Jill around Newport Beach harbor in our dinghy; had lunch at a sports bar and watched a football game; had a glass of wine on our hotel balcony while watching the sunset.

Riding around the harbor in our dinghy in Newport Beach

Tuesday: Attended an excellent biotech conference; went to "Taco Tuesday" at Sharkeez in Newport Beach with Jill and several friends. Ran on the boardwalk.

Wednesday: Biked to Dukes Restaurant with Jerry & Annie for dinner; Balboa Island walk after dinner.

Thursday: Sat next to the musician, Bertie Higgins, on the plane on the way back to Vancouver. We had a great conversation and developed a new friendship.

Friday: Morton's happy hour in Vancouver with Jill and friends from the office.

Saturday: Hiked up the Grouse Grind in North Vancouver with Jill and some friends, and had lunch and a few beers afterward; walked up to Robson Street in Vancouver and went out to dinner with Jill.

Sunday: Watched football; went hiking with Jill and Sunny at Lynn Valley in North Vancouver; rented a movie from Blockbuster.

Maybe you had two or three things in any one day that were fun, made you happy, relieved stress or were just "pleasant." Go ahead, write more than one thing. The goal is to identify everything that gave you positive feelings in today's environment. What is it that increased pleasure and fulfillment in your life under the current circumstances and with the current challenges you face? Go back and write down more as you think of them.

IMPORTANT POINT

Some people who read this list of my activities over the past week might think, "sure, I'd be happy too if I did all those things in a week."

This is exactly the point. Remember, the instructions for this exercise are to write down all the **positive** things you did or experienced. This does two things: (1) helps focus on the positives more than the negatives and (2) sets up a process for increasing the positive activities and experiences in your life.

This same week for me surely also had many difficult, stressful, and perhaps painful experiences. To BeHappy! we must not focus as much on these and, in fact, increase the number and effect of the great experiences and activities. This exercise starts the process of achieving that goal.

I make it a point to remember and record the positive experiences from everyday.

Another part of this process is to identify any common themes. You may have noticed some recurring activities in my list. For example, being outdoors shows up on my list several times in various ways — so it must be important to me. Spending time with my wife and friends is also a common theme and watching sports appears on my list more than once. Consequently, these must provide me some enjoyment or help make me happy and more fulfilled in my life **today**.

Are there any common themes in your list? If so, write them here:

•

•

•

•

STEP TWO: THE PAST MONTH

Assuming you were able to create a list of positive experiences from the past week, the next step is to go out a bit further by listing all the experiences from the past month that have made you "happy". Look at your calendar to jog your memory, go back over the past 30 days and recall what you have done, where you have been, who you spent time with, and what you have accomplished to help make you happy. Write everything you can recall here or in Apendix 3 (and use a separate sheet of paper if you need more space):

•

•

•

•

•

•

These were the experiences, activities, and events that have been positive for you in the past month, which are still related to your current situation. Maybe you had fun going to a movie or got satisfaction from completing a difficult project at work. Perhaps you were deeply fulfilled by going to one of your kid's events or had a spiritual experience hiking in the woods. Maybe it was just the relaxing feeling of reading a great book on a lazy Sunday afternoon or going shopping with some friends. Whatever you can think of that made you feel good, write it down in the spaces above. To provide you with some food for thought, here is my list for the past month:

Jill and Sunny playing in the snow in Vancouver.

- Went to the movies with Jill
- Biked around Stanley Park in Vancouver
- Played with Sunny in Lynn Valley Park
- Completed several important objectives and projects at the office
- Bought a great new jazz CD
- Rented 3 movies from Blockbusters
- Went to Whistler for a day of hiking
- Walked around Granville Island and had dinner on the patio at the Sandbar
- Took a great nap on Sunday afternoon
- Took Sunny to play in the snow
- Wrote a chapter in my next book
- Exchanged several e-mails with friends
- Ran 5 miles on the seawall in Stanley Park
- Went to dinner and a jazz club in Vancouver with friends

As with Step One (the 7-day review) you may detect some common themes during the past month, which represent positive factors in your life. Many could be quite simple things, like just relaxing or reading.

It doesn't matter what it is. It's only important at this stage of the process that you identify as many things as possible that affect your life in a positive way. We'll pull everything together later.

For example, I again see common themes in my list, such as spending time with my wife, accomplishments in my career, enjoying being with friends, being outdoors, writing, entertainment (movies and music) and traveling — all of which seem to come up often.

Write any common themes in my list from the past month here:

•

•

•

•

•

The impact here is two-fold. First, there are the actual events them-selves. Reflecting on the specific positive, fun, happy times of life helps iden-tify the kinds of things you like. Second, and just as important, is an aware-ness of what types of activities or events you remember, since these are the experiences that have the most positive impact on your life.

> **Key Point:** *Notice the pictures placed throughout this book. They are here for a reason. Pictures are a great tool to keep happiness in front of you constantly. This will be addressed more completely in Chapter Ten, "Some Extra Tools".*

STEP THREE: THE PAST YEAR

The next step is to go back even further in time, listing everything you can recall over the past year that has made you "happy". Again, use a calendar to go back one year from today. It may not be easy at first since many people find it difficult to remember what they did in the past 24 hours, but it's important since the intent here is to (a) identify what has made you happy during different times of your life and under different circumstances throughout your life, (b) recognize any trends during those years, and (c) uncover things that can be used later to increase your chances for lifelong happiness. This might take 15-30 minutes to complete. With the complexi-ties and stresses of everyday life today, it's easy to forget what made you happy in the past. This process will help you remember these important moments. So go ahead, write everything positive from the past year in the spaces below (or in Appendix 3):

-

-

-

-

-

Once again, to help your thinking process, here is my list for the past year:

- Catalina Island on our boat
- Scuba diving at Catalina Island
- Andy & Naida's Christmas Party in Tampa
- West Palm Music festival with friends
- Christmas with our families in Tampa

At Catalina Island on the boat.

- Super Bowl party in Newport Beach
- Skiing & snowboarding in Whistler
- Stayed debt-free
- Helped a friend decide on a career move and supported his change
- Newport Beach jazz concerts in the grass on Friday nights with Jerry and Annie
- Mediterranean cruise with friends
- Rented over 30 great movies
- Saved 40% of our after-tax income
- Achieved 8 of 11 corporate goals
- Went to the Cornucopia Wine Festival in Whistler with several friends
- Flew to Tampa on an urgent trip to attend the funeral of our good friend, Laura

This last entry may seem strange to you when you read it. Why would attending the funeral of a good friend be part of something that would lead to happiness? The answer is quite interesting, since it brings up some very important points about happiness and fulfillment. It relates to *contribution* (Chapter Ten), dealing with *adversity* (Chapter Eight), and avoiding *regret* (Chapter Nine).

Undoubtedly, the death of a good friend is a sad, traumatic experience. Even in times of intense emotional stress, however, we should still be able to BeHappy! (as described in Chapter One with the examples of Christopher Reeve and the death of my father).

Even an event like the death of a friend can lead to greater happiness in the long-term. Here's how: As mentioned, Laura was a long-time friend. Because of my career, my wife and I have been living in Vancouver, Canada for several years. Having grown up in Tampa, Florida, many of our friends live there. That included Laura. Just a few months before this particular week, unexpectedly, Laura was diagnosed with a form of lymphoma. She was only 36 years old. One weekend about four months after her diagnosis, we were in Whistler skiing and snowboarding, when we got an e-mail from one of our friends in Tampa telling us that Laura had taken a turn for the worse. A few days later, it was determined she wouldn't live more than another day or two at most. We were shocked, considering that the last report we had heard was that she was doing quite well. Once we heard this, we immediately started looking into plans to get to Tampa from Vancouver. Unfortunately we were told by our friends that the doctors felt she would not live through the night and it would be over by the time we would arrive in Tampa in a day or two. Even with this information, we decided to go anyway.

Interestingly, the doctors were wrong about the timing and Laura did not die right away as they expected. They had stopped feeding her and had even stopped giving her fluids for the entire previous week to prevent prolonging the process. For several days, everyone knew she only had a few hours left. We arrived two days later. We landed in Tampa airport at 8:00 PM on a Tuesday night, got picked up by some friends and went straight to the hospital. We arrived around 9:00 PM and were able to spend some time with

Laura before she died the next day. More importantly, Jill and I both believe Laura "felt" our presence that night and that she left us all the next day knowing even more than before that she was loved and cherished by many great friends. It was almost as if she had waited for all of us (her closest friends) to be together before she left us.

Dinner with some great friends in Tampa during Laura's last days with us.

We had made the right decision and had done the right thing. In some small way, we feel we contributed something positive to Laura's last few hours by showing her how much we cared. So, even with such an awful tragedy, it was awesome to feel we may have made a small difference. That feeling remains with us to this day and we are left with no *regrets* about the situation. We were also able to attend the funeral and be with our other friends during an extremely sad and difficult time for everyone, which helped us all cope a bit better.

Even though the incident was a major emotional trauma, the entire experience provided closure and comfort to us and many of our friends. It was a great feeling of contribution. Also, we will never have to live with a feeling of guilt or *regret* that we weren't there with her.

So, even negative emotional events can eventually play a part in our overall happiness — especially if there are long-lasting positive effects and a sense of contribution (however small or seemingly insignificant).

STEP FOUR: THE PAST DECADE

To this point you should have listed everything you could remember that has spiced up your life over the past 7 days, the past month, and the past year. If you have not finished, go back and do it now before moving on. If you have completed these first steps, next, to start understanding the positive emotions created during completely different times of your life — presumably when different circumstances existed — think about what you have done in the past 10 years that has made you "happy." What has made you proud over the past decade? What has given a sense of meaning, purpose, or gratitude? What have you contributed? What have you accomplished? With whom have you connected? How have you grown as a person?

Ask yourself the questions, where was I, what was I doing, who were my friends, and what were my favorite pastimes over the past decade? Think hard, and write down everything you can think of over the past ten years that made you happy or proud; everything that was fun, exciting, productive, interesting, enjoyable, pleasant, relaxing, fulfilling, etc. Include things that helped you become a better person. Write them all in the space below.

Jill winning Ms. Tampa Fitness context in 1995 (A great moment for her and a very proud moment for me).

-

-

-

-

-

-

STEP FIVE: HAPPINESS AS A CHILD

Over the past ten years your circumstances have most likely changed considerably. This may have become clear by completing the previous step. Have the things that made you happy ten years ago changed from the kinds of things you listed from the past week? Well, depending on your current age, things have probably changed even more dramatically since you were a child.

Our childhood years represent a completely different mindset from the way we think today. We had big dreams, endless possibilities, and few *rules*.

We were immortal! With that mindset, we were much more open and had much more opportunity to BeHappy!

Can you remember what made you happy as a child? Think back to when you were somewhere between 5 and 15 years of age. Come up with as many things as you can that contributed to making you happy back then. What were your *passions* and expectations for the future? It could have been a day with your family, playing on your little-league baseball team, being in a school play or anything that just

> *"One of the first things you can do to reconnect with your heart is to rekindle the passions that have died within you. Start doing the things that, in the past, filled up that big heart of yours. Begin to do what speaks to the passionate kid within you and makes you laugh so hard your belly hurts. Rediscover the things that move you and bring tears to your eyes."*
>
> — From "**The Saint, The Surfer, and The CEO**" by Robin Sharma

made you feel good. The more things you can remember, the better, so think hard. It is important to know what has made you happy in the past, at different points and under different circumstances, to be able to enjoy maximum happiness in the future because it helps better define your *identity* and your *passions*. If you are doing it right, you probably won't be able to keep from smiling. Even if you had a "tough childhood" and remember many negative things, there are always some positives if you think hard enough.

Young girls dancing on the beach.

Thinking about childhood and what made you happy when you were 7 or 8 years old can help get you back to the basic, simple truths about how to be happier as an adult because as children we really know how to BeHappy! We were good at it. We hadn't yet *learned* to be unhappy. We were less stressed and had less responsibility. We played and danced without being self-conscious. We laughed often

THINGS THAT COULD HAVE MADE YOU HAPPY AS A CHILD:

- ❑ *Throwing a baseball with your dad*
- ❑ *Helping your mom cook a great meal*
- ❑ *Getting together with friends after school*
- ❑ *Getting presents on your birthday*
- ❑ *Playing with your dog or cat*
- ❑ *Going on vacation with the family*
- ❑ *Building model airplanes*
- ❑ *Playing with dolls*
- ❑ *Playing video games*
- ❑ *Going to the beach*
- ❑ *Playing football*
- ❑ *Going to the store with your mother*
- ❑ *Going to your grandparent's*
- ❑ *Having dinner with the entire family*
- ❑ *Listening to the radio*
- ❑ *Playing an instrument*
- ❑ *Going to the ice cream store*
- ❑ *Going to Disneyland or Disney World*
- ❑ *Traveling somewhere in the car*
- ❑ *The feeling of doing well in school*
- ❑ *Playing with your brother or sister*
- ❑ *Writing*
- ❑ *Painting*
- ❑ *Singing*
- ❑ *Watching TV*
- ❑ *Dancing*
- ❑ *Playing music*
- ❑ *Going to school*
- ❑ *Playing board games*
- ❑ *Water skiing*
- ❑ *Going to the movies*
- ❑ *Making friends*
- ❑ *Reading*
- ❑ *Listening to music*
- ❑ *Collecting things*
- ❑ *Going to the zoo*
- ❑ *Working on a puzzle*
- ❑ *Playing a sport*
- ❑ *Drawing*
- ❑ *Snow skiing*
- ❑ *Playing cards*
- ❑ *Going fishing*

and were capable of dreaming big, regardless of the obstacles or challenges. We were curious and adventurous. All this because, as children, we hadn't yet learned to suppress our feelings, mold our desires to please others, or ignore our passions to conform to society, tradition, or a job. We also had not yet added many rules to our lives (we will discuss *rules* in Chapter Seven).

If you sit and watch children, notice how excited and happy they are most of the time. Try it sometime. It's hard not to wonder how we tend to mute this constant *passion* for life. As we grow up, we somehow become different from our true self, which can lead to internal conflict and some degree of unhappiness.

This part of the process has a goal: achieving happiness by recognizing that playful self you were as a child. It can lead to some significant insights.

Use the spaces below to list the things that you remember were positive, happy events or activities when you were a child. The box on the previous page lists some examples of activities or experiences that might have made you happy back then. Pick some of these if they apply to you, or even better, use this list only to spark your memory.

Write 5-10 things (more if possible) that made you happy as a child here:

-
-
-
-
-

STEP SIX: WHAT MAKES YOU UNHAPPY?

We need to do a few more things to complete this part of the journey. Just for a moment, we must explore the negative side of life. While it is generally not good to focus on the negatives, it is important to know what makes us unhappy in order to better understand what could make us happier in the future and avoid those things that can lead to unhappiness.

So, think of some of the negative aspects of the past 10 years. This may be easy for some, since many people dwell on the negatives in life anyway (which is part of the difficulty in being truly happy). If we could all simply dwell on the positives, we'd be way ahead. But for a moment, we will be thinking about the negative times. Specifically, what has been missing from your life in the past? What could have been better? How could you have enjoyed life more? What made you unhappy? What was unfulfilling? What do you *regret*? Write the answers to these questions or anything that comes to mind that made you unhappy in the past:

-
-
-
-

This part of the process could be difficult, since there may be some emotional or psychological pain associated with certain memories. There also may be many things you might have considered negative experiences as a child, but now realize they were really good things. Examples include going to school, practicing an instrument, or attending a house of worship. You may have once detested taking those piano lessons, but now you're glad you took them because you can make beautiful music for you and others to enjoy. So, if you listed some of these types of things and you really believe they were good things overall (for example, they were growth or learning experiences), then go back and cross those off the list.

Remember, in creating your personal *Happiness Plan* at the end of this book, many of the exercises completed in these initial chapters will be used as a basis for the plan. Everything, therefore,

SOME EXAMPLES OF WHAT COULD HAVE MADE YOU UNHAPPY IN THE PAST:

- Lying to someone
- Speaking in public
- Fighting with friends, siblings, or parents
- Going to the doctor
- Being "punished" for certain actions
- Being in the wrong relationship too long
- Getting divorced
- Not being honest with yourself
- Stealing something
- Hurting someone
- Killing an animal or insect
- Getting fired from a job
- Working in a job you hated
- Losing money in a poor investment
- Doing drugs
- Cheating on your spouse
- Seeing your parents argue
- Lacking integrity
- Being physically or sexually abused

could be important, so make sure to write down everything that comes to mind for now.

The box on the previous page contains some thought-provoking negative life events or experiences. Even something like "going to the doctor" could be psychologically important to avoid in the future. I know it is for me, and I am a physician. I know part of happiness for me when I am in my 80's and 90's will relate to my health and vitality.

Ideally, I never want to have to take medication or make frequent doctor visits. To achieve this I must stay healthy. There are many things I can do now, therefore, as part of my action plan to happiness that could give me a better chance of eliminating this negative occurrence from my later life. Obviously, everyone is different. For some people, going to the doctor may have been a positive, supportive experience in the past and will not negatively affect happiness in the future.

> *"If sunsets make you happy, then you'll be happy at least once almost everyday."*
>
> **—Yanni**

STEP SEVEN: WHAT WILL MAKE YOU HAPPY IN THE FUTURE?

Finally, we must look ahead. Many things that made us happy in the past may not make us happy in the future. We now need to identify what could be used to make you happier in the future, using everything completed so far as a basis. While this was begun in Chapter One when you created your *Definition of Happiness*, doing it again now after remembering the positives and negatives about your past could provide some additional support and a better indication of what will make you happier in the future. In fact, it may even be a little different from what you thought would make you happy in the future if you had not first looked at the past.

So, think about where you see yourself five years from now. What will you be doing? What do you want to be doing?

Sunset over Catalina Island.

With whom will you be spending time (or with whom would you like to be spending time)? Where do you want to live? What will make you happy in 5 years? What will make you more fulfilled, complete, and satisfied? What career will you be pursuing? How do you picture your financial situation? What are your goals? Write down as many things as possible (and stay within the next five years):

•

•

•

•

•

Now, what about in twenty years? Where will you be twenty years from today? What will you be doing? How, and with whom, will you be spending

> "People overestimate what they can do in a year and underestimate what they can do in ten years."
>
> —*Tony Robbins*

your time? Is this different from the answers for five years? What do you want for your financial status and your career? And, given this vision of your future, what will make you happy? Write down the things that come to your mind, and be as specific as possible.

In 20 years…

•

•

•

•

•

STEP EIGHT: PUTTING IT ALL TOGETHER

With the information created in this chapter, it is important to summarize your thoughts and identify the most important elements of the joy, fulfillment, happiness, and pain you have experienced in your life. To do this, first go back through each section in this chapter and review the common themes again. Go back to Step One (pp. 34–35), which lists situations from the past 7 days and see what comes up more than once (like spending time with your spouse, the outdoors, traveling, or being with friends). If you don't have any repeats or any common themes, don't worry. It isn't essential. Just list the one or two most important or significant things you identified.

Now, go through the past month (pp. 37–38), the past year (pp. 39–40), and the past decade (pp. 42–43) and write down all the common themes or most significant issues in the spaces below.

-
-
-
-
-
-

If you found any common themes or major positive factors, the basic goal will be to focus more on these types of activities, emotions, and feelings in the future, and include them regularly in your daily life. This is what you like to do, what creates your *identity*, or what provides fulfillment — all of which can help lead to greater happiness. It is not necessarily what will make you happy overall, but these things can help make you happier in the short-term while you work more on the long-term. It will be part of your *Happiness Plan* and, in some ways, really helps define who you are as a person — which is another significant component of happiness as addressed in Chapter Two.

Once the entire system is in place, and you have all the tools you need for being happier, the challenge will be to avoid as many of the negatives as possible. If you find some common themes, make sure they are clearly listed in the spaces above. If you find no common themes, write down anything from the positive lists you created earlier in this chapter — the ones that give you the greatest sense of joy, fulfillment, and/or pleasure. Find at least one and then write it down in the spaces above.

Don't worry. If you feel this seems somewhat superficial and these relatively minor things could not lead to true happiness, you are partially right. There is much more to it. As is the case with many other things in life, it is important to start with the basics and work through the process in a systematic way, building upon each with every step of the journey. And, like most "transformations" (which is what this could be for you), it doesn't typically happen quickly. It evolves through a series of well-planned, effective actions that lead to the end result.

As an overall summary of this part of the system, let's organize each of the major points. Re-write your *Definition of Happiness* again. Yes, one more time. Go back to the *definition* you created in Chapter One. Revise it if necessary, based on what you have discovered in the 8-step process just completed. Write your *definition* here:

Now, what are the major things that have made you unhappy in the past? List up to 3 here:

•

•

•

These are the types of experiences to avoid in the future. We will get to how that is done in Chapter Eleven as you create your personal *Happiness Plan*.

At this point, list the top five most important experiences or activities that have made you happy in the past — all the way back, from your childhood to events of the past week:

•

•

•

•

•

Obviously you want more of these types of experiences and activities in your life. Some of them may even need to become part of your regular routine. So, reflect on some of the details of this chapter. Pull out some *pictures* of happy times, fun moments, and fulfilling situations or accomplishments in your life. Consider the things you can appreciate about your life right now — even if life is currently very difficult for you.

By creating a way to constantly remind yourself of how many good things exist in your life, you can begin to be more grateful and appreciative. Focus everyday on some aspect of the positive situations. Think about how you can include more of these positives in your life and start eliminating some of the negatives. It is not an easy task. It will take commitment and a proactive approach to achieve the best result possible — but it will be well worth it.

CHAPTER SUMMARY & KEY POINTS

1. Knowing what has made you happy and unhappy in the past, at different times in your life, can help create more happiness in the future.

2. As children, we really know how to BeHappy! We learn to be unhappy as we go through life and become adults.

3. In creating your Happiness Plan, it is important that you fulfill your *Definition of Happiness*. Knowing specifically what kinds of things made you happy throughout your life can help create a better plan.

PART TWO

Essential Elements

With the foundation now built through the concepts and exercises in Part One, there are three critical factors to address which can effect our happiness in life, both positively and negatively. These essential elements are (1) relationships, (2) health, and (3) money. By understanding these three elements thoroughly, we can create true fulfillment through lasting relationships, great health, and financial security.

4

RELATIONSHIPS: THE ULTIMATE "HAPPINESS LOOP"

OBJECTIVES OF THIS CHAPTER

- To understand how important happiness is to developing great relationships.
- An introduction to the "Happiness Loop".
- To learn how to create better relationships.
- Learning to nurture your relationships as a key to lifelong happiness.

EARLIER IN THE BOOK, it was suggested that your journey toward happiness, like most other trips, requires a map. Your map will be created fully in Chapter Eleven using the tools, ideas and concepts from the first ten chapters. At this point, however, there are some basic essentials, which must be addressed before embarking. And, more than anything in this book, the concepts and tools in this chapter can change your life completely.

Relationships, the first essential component of happiness, can make the difference between reaching your destination and getting lost. It can also determine how much you enjoy the trip.

Even more than health and money, *relationships* have the greatest potential to affect our happiness both positively and negatively. So, if there were a way to find, build, and maintain better, more fulfilling relationships…would you be interested?

This refers to all types of relationships, including romantic or intimate relationships (usually with one special person), close personal connections (like those with family and friends), and business associations with colleagues, partners or teammates. All are essential to achieving true happiness, even if your *Definition of Happiness* includes nothing about relationships. The reason for this is simple. *Relationships* have the power to make us happy or unhappy, regardless of everything else going on in our lives.

It is very common to see wealthy people who are miserable because they are in the wrong relationships. Many fit, healthy people are depressed because they don't get along with their families. Even some of the most powerful people on earth are not happy because they have no real friends. What this implies is that wealth, health, and power alone cannot make people happy.

On the other hand, there are many people who have very little financially or who are in poor health (perhaps, even terminally ill) and are still fundamentally happy because of the love and support they get from one special person, their families, and/or many great friends. There are countless examples of normal, everyday people who are much happier than the most famous, powerful people simply because they derive all the important "juice" they need in life from their spouse, children, family and friends.

Yes, relationships can be the most powerful force in the quest for happiness.

Special relationships are powerful.

THE "HAPPINESS LOOP"

Since relationships are so essential to happiness, the topic is the first and most important part of this "essential elements" section. In fact, just as you cannot take a cross-country trip without a good, reliable vehicle, you will get nowhere on this trip to complete happiness without strong, solid relationships.

What is both interesting and challenging about this component of our life is that the connection between relationships and happiness is a "chicken-and-egg" situation. In other words, which comes first? While great relationships will make you happier, being happy will also help you create great relationships since it provides the catalyst required to initiate and maintain better relationships. I call it a "Happiness Loop", which looks something like this:

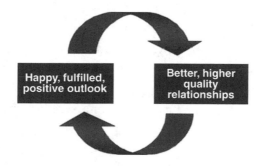

ENTERING THE HAPPINESS LOOP

There is nothing more attractive than a happy person, and in fact, unhappy people are generally not very "attractive" at all (except maybe to other unhappy people). Even unhappy people, however, are "happier" in the company of other unhappy people (you may have heard the saying "misery loves company").

My very good friend, Jeff, has said to me, "If you had met me a few years earlier than you did, we would probably never have become friends." The reason is simple: he was not very happy at the time and so he would not have been as "attractive" to me as a potential friend. This unhappiness related mostly to his career at the time. It was inconsistent with his *identity* and he was miserable. Fortunately, he had an

> *"There is nothing more attractive than a happy person"*
>
> **—Author Unknown**

outstanding *relationship* with his wife, Patty, who helped keep him some-what balanced, and supported his decision to make a change. He started a new career and changed his life completely. He even quit smoking since it was also inconsistent with his *identity* once he became happier. I feel very lucky that he changed his life since he is now one of the happiest people I know and he and Patty are amongst our closest friends, providing **us** much happiness over the past twenty years.

The point is this: one of the best ways to have great relationships is to BeHappy! And one of the best ways to BeHappy! is to have great relationships. That is the "loop".

To manage this cycle, like many things in life, you must be proactive. Knowing who you are, what you want, and how you are committed to liv-ing your life — as defined in the last two chapters — are key starting points. From there, it is critical to understand the process of creating and main-taining great relationships, and then making sure you manage your rela-tionships continuously.

In other words, being happy, positive and fulfilled will help create bet-ter, higher quality relationships because you will be more attractive to the right people for you. As a consequence, having more high quality relation-ships will give you a happier, more fulfilled, positive outlook, moving the cycle in the positive direction and generating momentum.

> **Key Point:** *The best way to have great relationships is to* BeHappy!

Of course, just being happy is not enough. This is just a start to the process. Once you have established some great relationships, it takes work to maintain them. More on this later — for now, since this book is not intend-ed to help you find your perfect relationship(s), the strategy for our pur-poses is to help you "enter the loop" by becoming happier and more fulfilled first, thereby fueling the cycle toward better relationships; which will then bring even more happiness to your life.

In other words, the goal is to use the tools and concepts in this book to become happier, which will result in improved relationships. In fact, a great side effect of this book may end up being a great new relationship with someone. You may even find your soul mate — if you haven't already — all because you are a happier, more attractive person, open to the right person for you.

So the first objective is to get as much out of this book as possible by committing to the process; because if you do you will be a much happier person, which will make you more "attractive". It's actually better than plastic surgery!

Pictured here is part of an advertisement for a dating service — which is a multi-billion dollar industry. Many people are looking for the "right" relationship and they are willing to pay for it. The dating and relationship industries know this. They advertise what I call the "back end" of the happiness loop. They suggest that, by using their service, you will find the right person for you, which will make you happy — like the couple in the ad. And, they are partially right: the **right** relationship(s) **will** make you happier.

> **Key Point:** *Being happy will make you more "attractive" and can facilitate your entry into the relationship "Happiness Loop".*

The truth is, however, it becomes much easier to attract and develop the right relationships if you are happy first — truly happy (the "front end" of the happiness loop). Even a dating service could fail to help you meet the person you desire if you are not already happy, since you will not be as attractive to that type of person. You may find someone as unhappy as you. Even if you were to meet the "right person", the relationship would likely not last.

You have surely heard of people who keep getting into the wrong relationships. They just keep attracting the wrong people into their lives. While there are many reasons for this, one reason is their own attitude. They are not totally happy, so they attract unhappy, negative people.

Yes, the happiness loop works quite well in reverse. In fact, it can even be more efficient than the positive direction. In other words, the less happy a person is, the weaker their relationships will tend to be. If they do form new relationships, they will generally not be positive, fulfilling relationships. They will probably even lose some of the good relationships they have. Poor relationships usually lead to deeper unhappiness — ultimately ending up many times in loneliness, low self-esteem, and even depression.

So you can see why it is so crucial to keep this loop moving in the positive direction. The only way to make that happen is to BeHappy! and stay happy — largely by using the techniques found in this book. By using these tools consistently, there will be no opportunity for significant negativity to upset the forces that make up happiness, which will result in better relationships and continually increasing happiness.

If you are already very happy and have many great relationships, it is extremely important to nurture these relationships since all relationships require effort. This includes the relationship with one special person as well as relationships with friends and family.

Even more importantly, if you are not very happy right now — and are fortunate enough to have some great relationships in your life — it is criti-

> **Key Point:** *Happiness is the fuel for the relationship "Happiness Loop".*

cal to do *whatever it takes* to nurture and maintain them before they are ruined (an inevitable consequence of negativity and unhappiness).

By being happy, people will be naturally attracted to you, so your happiness is the fuel for this relationship-happiness cycle. It is then up to you to take the next step, which, in the case of friends and family relationships, includes regular contact (phone calls, letters, e-mails, and personal visits) and some degree of contribution. Generally, just your contribution of time, appreciation, and thought is enough. It's typically the little things that can make a big difference.

So, call the people closest to you regularly. Go to lunch with a different friend or family member once a month. Even an e-mail once in a while can help show you care. Nurture your relation-

> *"Without friends, no one would choose to live, though he had all other goods." —Aristotle*

Important Exercise: To really be proactive about this, make a list of the people whose relationships are most important to you. Use the spaces below and place each person's name in the appropriate category:

Immediate Family	Extended Family	Friends	Business and Other

These are the people you cherish most as family, friends, associates, and teammates.

Now, list the top two or three in each category and design a way to nurture each relationship — something you can do immediately to contribute to that person's life in a way that shows you care about them and your relationship. Use the space below and a separate sheet if necessary:

ships and you will be happier. Lose them and you will be less happy. It is really a simple formula. Give it a try.

MARRIAGE (OR THE EQUIVALENT) AND CHILDREN

For many people, the most important relationships related to happiness are those involving one special person — ideally a "soul mate" — and/or their children.

In a special one-on-one relationship — like marriage for example — it is critically important to nurture the relationship to keep it solid and growing. If you are in such a relationship, you probably listed that person above. And everyone who is in such a relationship, no matter how good it is, knows it requires work to maintain and grow. Being happy is essential.

A happy, passionate, positive attitude forms the basis for a healthy relationship, assuming you are in such a relationship with the right person. And if you are, you must continuously nurture the relationship (and in this case, e-mails and lunches are not enough). For example, you must make your spouse or "significant other" feel special and important by showing them regularly. It means doing little things that make a difference. Most importantly, your happiness will help keep the relationship positive.

> **Key Point:** *The best way to find and keep your soul mate is to* BeHappy!

As an additional exercise, therefore, for those of you who are married or have a special one-on-one relationship, create a list of at least ten ideas you can use to make this person feel special on a regular basis:

1.

2.

3.

4.

5.

6.

7.

8.

9.

10.

Use this list — and your positive attitude — to help keep your special relationship strong.

For those with children, a strong bond is generally a critical factor in your ability to **BeHappy!** This is, therefore, another important relationship to nurture and develop.

It may be even more important than you may think at first. Because in reality, your happiness is just as important for the proper growth and development of your children as it is for your own life. So, for those of you with children, if their personality, integrity, and character are important to you (which for most parents it is the number one priority), perhaps this provides even more incentive for you to be as happy as possible. Yes, the contribution you will make to your children by being happy is huge.

If you need coaching on what it takes to nurture and maintain a marriage or a strong relationship with your children, there are many books on the subject. One of the books coming to this **BeHappy!** series is **BeTogether!**, which will get more specific on these important topics. For this book, however, the objective is to make you aware of how happiness will allow you to create higher quality relationships, which will then make you even happier in your life. This "Happiness Loop" concept is the key.

GETTING LUCKY

While managing the front end of the happiness loop (i.e., being happy) is the best way to create many great relationships, sometimes people get lucky. They may be unhappy or down and along comes their soul mate — someone who is positive, happy, and perfect for them. They are in the right place at the right time and it just happens, despite their negative emotional state. If this occurs, everything can turn around, even if this soul mate is also not completely happy. The movie, *The Cooler*, with William Macy and Alex Baldwin is a great example. In the movie, everything changes for Macy, who is really unhappy, when he meets his soul mate and falls in love, even though she is not very happy either. As soon as the relationship develops, his life changes, his personality changes, even his relationships with others changes — all because of the new relationship in his life. It is a dramatic transformation.

> *"The supreme happiness of life is the conviction that we are loved"*
>
> —*Victor Hugo*

The point of this chapter, then, is to make you aware of the existence of this happiness loop so you can (a) use the tools in the book to make you more attractive to the right people for you and (b) create and maintain the right relationships, thereby increasing your ability to be even happier.

Here's an illustration of the true power of relationships. Have you known an elderly person who has died within a relatively short time after the death of their spouse? It happens quite frequently, and although it can be related to several factors, it can be influenced greatly by the impact of the loss of the relationship.

This is how powerful it can be. It is one of the fundamental, foundational aspects of happiness, so take it seriously. BeHappy! and you will create some beautiful, lasting, fulfilling relationships. Then, these great relationships will allow you to really BeHappy! What a deal!

One final thought about relationships … for those who use movies as entertainment and learning, watch *Elizabethtown* and *It's a Wonderful Life*. Just do it — you'll see why.

CHAPTER SUMMARY & KEY POINTS

1. Great, fulfilling relationships will make you happier. The more the better.

2. A "Happiness Loop" exists, fueled first by being happy, which makes you more "attractive" to the right people and expands your relationship potential.

3. If you have some great relationships in your life right now, whether you are happy or not, you must do whatever it takes to maintain and nourish them.

4. An outstanding intimate relationship (like a great marriage) can make you happier than you ever thought possible, especially if you have found your soul mate. The best way to find your soul mate is to BeHappy!

5. If you are in a solid one-on-one relationship, like a marriage, you must also manage and nurture it continuously.

6. A great source of happiness for many people is children, and your happiness is critical to the proper development of those children.

5

BeHappy!
TO BE HEALTHY

OBJECTIVES OF THIS CHAPTER

- To help understand the link between health and happiness.
- To introduce the concept that being happy can actually lead to better health.
- To increase your incentive to use the tools and concepts in this book to be happier

---

IT'S PROBABLY NOT DIFFICULT to understand the concept that the healthier you are, the happier you can be. Most people would not argue with that statement. It's a fairly simple concept. It is clear, however, that many unhappy people are perfectly healthy and many happy people are not completely healthy. Deviating, therefore, from the conventional thinking about health and happiness, this chapter addresses an alternative concept, namely, BeHappy! *and you can be healthier.* Looking at it this way can create a greater incentive or reason to use the tools in this book to BeHappy! (very similar to the situation with *relationships* described in Chapter Four).

I realize some readers may feel the notion that *happiness can make you healthier* is a bit far-fetched, and although I am a physician and have a taken a professional oath to improve people's health, my objective is not to convince you of my beliefs. My primary goal in writing this book was to help you become as happy as possible. So, if I can provide a way to influence your actions toward a life filled with more happiness, I will have succeeded. If you use the information in this book, however, and better health is a side effect, then my mission as a physician is also met (which is one of the criteria for my *purpose* in life) — which makes me even happier!

Although not quite as powerful, this is somewhat similar to the "Happiness Loop" concept presented in Chapter Four — where it was revealed that great *relationships* lead to increased happiness, and increased happiness leads to better relationships. Similarly, what I am proposing here is that good health leads to increased happiness and increased happiness leads to better health. I say it is not quite as powerful because it seems people can still BeHappy! even with major physical challenges or health problems (as was the case with Christopher Reeve) but they cannot generally BeHappy! when their relationships are poor. And, although the association between health and happiness is not quite as powerful as the connection between relationships and happiness, the link between psychology and physiology (health) is extremely powerful and well documented in the scientific literature.

During my career as a practicing physician, it became clear that a significant percentage of the people I treated for **physical** illnesses were actually experiencing manifestations of **psychological** influences. Don't get me wrong; I am not saying unhappiness *causes* cancer, diabetes, or hypertension. What I am saying, however, is that consistent and long-term negative psychological influences or stresses — like significant worry, regret or anxiety — can affect health in major ways; including making your body more vulnerable to disease. The opposite is also true. A consistent, positive emotional state (i.e., happiness) can foster improved health by creating a more robust internal physiological environment that can actually prevent disease.

Fundamentally, in my years in medical practice I observed that stressed, frustrated, unfulfilled people tend to get more diseases than balanced, happy, fulfilled people. In addition, it is obvious that people with diseases or general poor health are not as happy as people who are healthy, fit, and vibrant.

As with the previous chapter on *relationships*, the objective of this chapter is to help make you a happier person first, which in turn can improve your health (as it can for your *relationships*). Improvements in your *health* and your *relationships* will then help make you a happier person. It is a great self-perpetuating "happiness machine". So if you can keep your mind open to the possibility that happiness could create better *health*, there could be even greater incentives to use the tools this book has to offer.

> **Key Point:** *If happiness can actually lead to good health, why not choose to be happy? If it can't, then why not be happy anyway? It's a no lose situation.*

As an extreme example, you may have heard of cases where terminal cancer patients were completely cured by laughter. I know it sounds impossible. But it has happened and, once again, remember — *Nothing is Impossible.*[5] This concept is documented in the medical literature and supported through a more subtle example in a 2004 study published in the *New England Journal of Medicine*, which demonstrates that people who are "grateful" live longer than people who are not. And gratitude is one of the major influencers of happiness.

Although my medical training was not focused on psychology or psychiatry, much of my medical practice dealt with physical disease as a manifestation of psychological pain or stress. It is amazing how so much of the illness we see in medicine can be linked to psychological origins.

A practical example of the impact psychology has on physiology is the very real "placebo effect". You may have heard of this. It relates to the effect an inert or inactive substance has on a disease or physical condition. The US FDA uses it routinely in clinical trials to help determine the true effect of a drug, and in fact, comparison to placebo is generally a requirement for approval of a drug.

> **Key Point:** *Much of the cause of sickness and disease is a manifestation of psychological stress.*

The placebo effect exists, regardless of the condition or disease. Whether it is hypertension, diabetes, or even cancer, a certain percentage of people in clinical trials conducted by pharmaceutical and biotech companies show improvements in their condition — or may even be "cured" — by a placebo (i.e., a sugar pill), which may relate partially to psychology.

In other words, some people in these trials just believe they are on an active drug and get better. For others, their body may heal itself, perhaps by an improvement in their immunity related to the new positive psychology or sense of hope and optimism the "drug" provides. Whatever the cause, somehow the positive psychological effects related to taking something these people believe will make them better, helps create an internal physiological environment that allows the body to respond better to the disease. It is another well-documented fact.

More anecdotal, but just as remarkable, are the fairly frequent cases where "attitude" has an effect on a terminal disease. A friend shared one such example with me. One of his friends was diagnosed with terminal cancer and was told he had less than six months to live. Upon learning this, he quit his job, went snow skiing for months at a time (one of his passions), and generally lived "all out", doing whatever he felt like doing, whenever he felt like doing it. After all, what did he have to lose? He wanted to live out his remaining few months completely as he pleased. That was several years ago and he is still alive. Could this be a fluke or coincidence? Sure it could. But there are many cases like this where evidence exists for a major link between psychology and physiology. It is similar to the concept I mentioned previously in which many people who retire or lose a spouse tend to die within a relatively short time. It relates to some extent to psychology.

Again, this may seem unbelievable. Having been trained as a physician, it is certainly difficult for me to buy totally into the concept. But after seeing tens of thousands of patients and thousands of diseases in my medical career, I became convinced that psychology effects physiology, both directly and indirectly. And as I stated before, my goal is not to get you to believe what I believe. My goal is to make you happier. Being healthy is one way to be happier, and being happy is one way to be healthier.

So, regardless of your beliefs on the subject, it is safe to assume you believe that being happy is better than being unhappy. Who knows? You may just get some unexpected health benefits later in life.

A MORE TRADITIONAL EXAMPLE RELATED TO THE SUBJECT OF HEALTH, HAPPINESS, AND BALANCE...

It is well documented that obesity contributes to a variety of diseases such as diabetes, hypertension (high blood pressure), heart attack and stroke. It is a major health problem, especially in the United States. So, if you are overweight, losing some of that weight and achieving your ideal body weight could help you avoid the future pain and suffering associated with these life-threatening conditions. This alone could make you happier later in life.

*One way to maintain your ideal body weight is to adhere to a **generally** healthy diet. It has many positive benefits. Even so, it is also important to enjoy the process, so it is good to take pleasure in the positive emotional and social benefits food and drink can offer. As with all things in life, balance is important, with proper nutrition preferably making up a higher proportion of your life. For example, I love pizza, beer, and nachos every once in a while. These are generally considered not to be very healthy foods. But having these occasionally helps me enjoy life a little more, and so as long as my usual diet consists of healthy, nutritious foods that help keep me close to my ideal body weight and physiological balance, I can live a happy, healthy life.*

Maintaining an ideal body weight provides many psychologically advantages as well as the health benefits. It can lead to better self-esteem, greater confidence, and an overall sense of pride and well being. So maintaining an ideal weight, along with a regular exercise program can be a tremendous psychological boost since exercise has been shown to reduce stress and can help promote a sense of accomplishment and growth.

This example addresses the common point that better health leads to happiness, and as a physician, I know how difficult and stressful it is to be ill. I saw it everyday in my medical practice. The frequent doctor visits, medication requirements, and constant sick feeling are all very painful. Even the potential financial implications could be a major burden.

*These are standard and accepted concepts. And, they are very important to the primary objective of this book, which is to make you as happy as possible, regardless of your circumstances or challenges. What becomes even more critical (and more in line with the point of this chapter) are the **psychological** benefits exercise and proper nutrition can create in preventing serious long-term **physiological** conditions.*

So maintain good health and you can be happier. Also, BeHappy! to BeHealthy!

CHAPTER SUMMARY & KEY POINTS

1. Although it may difficult to comprehend, it is possible that happiness can lead to better health (the reverse is also true — unhappiness can lead to poorer health).

2. The "placebo effect" is a real phenomenon used to evaluate the validity of human clinical trials, providing evidence that psychology relates closely to physiology.

3. BeHappy! and, perhaps, you'll be healthier (and live longer).

6

MONEY AND HAPPINESS

OBJECTIVES OF THIS CHAPTER

- To understand how money can influence happiness.
- Making sure money is not a deterrent to happiness, regardless of your financial situation.

IF YOU'VE SEEN THE MOVIE, *It's A Wonderful Life* (my personal favorite) you may remember the part where George Bailey (played by Jimmy Stewart) has just met Clarence, his guardian angel. Clarence has been sent down from heaven to save George's life. George is in the midst of a financial crisis to the point where he is about to commit suicide. In response to his guardian angel's request to help him, George, who doesn't believe Clarence is an angel, sarcastically asks him if he has "a spare $8,000", since that's what would help him most at the moment. Clarence explains to George that there is no money in heaven, to which George responds: "Well it comes in pretty handy down here, Bub".

Most would agree that money does come in pretty handy (in a majority of cultures, at least). Much of our culture seems to revolve around money and wealth. But, can money make us happy? Even though many of us are taught that money cannot make us happy, I believe the real answer to that question is both "YES" and "NO."

While money itself cannot make most people happy, the 'yes' part of the answer comes from the fact that money can be a "means to an end" — especially if your *Definition of Happiness* from Chapter One includes things money can provide. Also, significant financial stress (i.e., lack of money) can lead to unhappiness for many people.

Unfortunately, many people have the belief that money can actually lead to unhappiness. In reality, financial abundance (i.e., having enough money to do

> *"Wealth is a means to an end, not the end itself. As a synonym for health and happiness, it has had a fair trial and failed dismally"*
>
> —*John Galsworth*

what you want, when you want) can provide us with more tools with which to BeHappy! At the very least, it could provide some degree of peace of mind and can be a great source of *contribution*. And, if part of your *Definition of Happiness* includes financial abundance, financial independence, or financial security, then it will be more important to your happiness as compared to those whose definition does not include a financial component.

I include money in this Essential Elements section of the book, therefore, because it is a factor — to some degree — in everyone's life. And, money (it's lack or abundance) could determine the degree to which you are able to achieve true happiness.

As part of my research for this book, I asked many people who felt they were already happy, "what would make you even happier?" Many of the answers I got were related to "more travel," "more free time," and "doing more of what I love to do." Also, "less stress" came up as a frequent answer. All of these could be made more possible with more money.

Have you ever heard someone say they would love to go somewhere (like Europe) or do something (like take a cruise) but they can't afford it? Sure you have.

I love to travel, for example. It's one of the things that showed up quite often on my lists of what made me happy in the past week, the past month, the past year, and even as a young child. But travel can be expensive, so more money allows me to travel more — which fulfills my needs and makes me happier. Also, for several years, my wife and I lived on a yacht in southern California with our dog, Stoley. It was a tremendous experience that I highly recommend to anyone who values adventure in their lives (in fact, we named the boat *What A Life!*). To this day, I consider it one of the best periods of time in my life. To me, there is nothing better than being out on a beautiful day, cruising the Pacific Ocean and spending time at Catalina Island with my wife and our dog; enjoying the cool, clear water and basking in the warm sun, reading a great book or even working. It improves my quality of life and makes me "happy." All this, however, requires a certain amount of money. Yachts are typically

fairly expensive. Even fuel and maintenance are quite costly — especially with gas prices as they are these days.

Could I BeHappy! without these things? Sure! But something would be missing from my life if I couldn't afford them. Also, since financial abundance is part of my *Definition of Happiness*, I would likely not be completely happy without a certain level of financial success. Money adds to my happiness because it gives me the ability to do more of the things that add adventure and variety to my life, which are important to me — as seen in the examples in Chapter Three of what has made me happy in the past. It also provides me significant peace-of-mind, since being financially stretched is stressful for me. These are all part of my *Definition of Happiness*. It may or may not be part of yours.

Some of this surely relates to my past since while I was growing up, our family didn't have much money. My father, a pharmacist making less than

---

Key Point: *If money and/or the things money can provide make up part of your **Definition of Happiness**, it is important to have a plan to achieve a certain degree of wealth to* BeHappy! *In this way, money can augment your happiness.*

about $25,000 per year in those days, had to work three jobs at times just to support our family of six. He wanted a boat so badly he could taste it. Not a big one either; just a 15-17 footer to be able to go fishing or cruising on the one Saturday a month he had off from work. But he could never afford it. Sure, he had other sources of happiness in his life — like his children — but more money would have certainly enhanced the quality of his life — even if just to make him feel he was providing a better life for us. As I mentioned previously, he died of pneumonia at the age of 57, never having had the experience of freedom, adventure, or peace of mind that a bit more wealth could have brought him. And, reflecting on the *happiness-health* concept from Chapter Five, I wonder if this could have been a factor in his early death? After he died, one thing I wished for my mother was that she would get the opportunity to live life with more abundance. That wish has been granted and I believe she is happier for it, even though she lost her husband (my father) years ago. She has been able to travel to Europe and other places several times, something she was never able to do before. She even found a new relationship, her husband Gabe, who enriched her life tremendously.

So, while money itself will not make us happy if we are unhappy, depending on what we want in life, it could allow us to go more places, do more things, have more freedom and adventure, or contribute more to our family, friends, and society. In addition, financial pressures increase stress. Marriages have failed because of it. People have even committed suicide due to financial difficulties.

> *Key Point: While money and wealth can help augment happiness if used properly, it will not compensate for bad relationships, poor health, or living out of sync with your identity.*

This book is not designed to help you create wealth. That will be the subject of one of my future books, called **BeWealthy!** Rather, this chapter is intended to address the degree to which financial abundance can assist you in your quest for more happiness. So, for our purposes here, you must determine the degree to which money plays a role in your life through your

Definition of Happiness and commit to a plan to get to where you need to be financially to be as happy as possible. In other words, depending on your current situation and the *Definition of Happiness* you created in Chapter One, there may or may not be things you need to do to improve your financial position. Getting to that financial level is a completely separate process.[6] The steps are basically the same as the steps to becoming happier, beginning with defining what you want and where you are, and then developing a plan on how to get there.

IF YOU DON'T HAVE (OR DON'T WANT) AN ABUNDANCE OF MONEY...

Everyone is capable of improving their financial position and even becoming financially independent (wealthy). However, not everyone knows how, or even wants it. While it is not the objective of this book to make people wealthier, the goal **is** to help make you happy regardless of your circumstances, financial or otherwise. That is what this chapter and the others in this book will help you achieve.

> *"The happiest people don't necessarily have the best of everything; they just make the best of everything."*
>
> —*Anonymous*

Some people do not want to be wealthy. It may not be part of your *Definition of Happiness*. You may even feel that wealth is bad. Regardless of your opinion, however, the good news is that to be totally happy, you do not have to be rich. I know from personal experience that you can have very little money and also be very happy. As stated in the previous sections of this chapter, however, money helps provide additional tools toward happiness if it is an important component of your *definition*, or if it helps contribute to that *definition* in some way.

For example, I recall when I was in medical school: I was about 20 years old and was what most people would consider financially "poor". I was also very happy. Maybe you can relate.

Was there a time in your life when you were happiest? Were you any better off financially than you are today? If not, what was the difference? For me, there were four things that made me happy, even though I could barely make ends meet.

Those were:

1. Having a significant goal and a positive expectation for the future

2. Managing expectations

3. Staying out of debt

4. Appreciating what I had

With this happiness, I also enjoyed the "richness" of many great *relationships* (as described in Chapter Four).

Let's explore each of the points above individually.

HAVING A SIGNIFICANT GOAL AND POSITIVE EXPECTATION FOR THE FUTURE...

Having a major goal (or several goals) creates hope and possibility. For me, back when I was in medical school, I obviously had a goal to become a physician. That goal was exciting and motivating (two great emotions that can foster happiness). Even though I was living in a small, drab apartment, had little money for food — much less for extras, the goals and expectations I had for the future made me love life and its possibilities. Hope, possibility, and direction can help create positive energy, motivation, and excitement; which are all part of the general emotion we call happiness.

Statistics indicate that many people die within a few years of retirement. Why is that? Partly, I believe, is because for many people a significant amount of possibility and direction has been removed from their lives when they retire (especially if retirement is not their choice). Although not as powerful, it is somewhat akin to the common phenomenon mentioned in the chapter on relationships, where some elderly people tend to die soon after the death of a spouse.

To create and maintain happiness, then, it is important to continuously build hope and possibility into your life. You must have a direction. And, consistent with that direction, you must have some short, medium, and long-term goals (see Chapter Ten, page 132 for more details on goals). Also, having a *purpose* in life or personal mission statement could be important, as described in Chapter Two.

So as a start, answer this question: What is possible in your future? Again, don't hold back because of limiting beliefs or current circumstances. What is really possible for you? Is it massive financial success or significant career advancement? Is it that your child becomes a happy, successful person? Is it that you create a legacy? What about who you can become as a person or what you can *contribute*?

Write down or list the answers in the spaces below:

What is possible in your future?

•

•

•

•

If you really thought about this question — really listing what is possible in your life, you should have felt a sense of hope and excitement just by thinking about it and writing it down. Listing these possibilities for your future — especially if you really consider the opportunities and visualize the outcome, should make you feel motivated and optimistic since it can represent personal growth and opportunity. All these emotions, if created and maintained daily, will make you happier regardless of how much or little money you have. This will be included in your *Happiness Plan*.

MANAGING EXPECTATIONS

Most people know someone who has very little money and is also very happy.

> *"Success is not the key to Happiness. Happiness is the key to success"*
>
> —*Albert Schweitzer*

I assume you know someone who seems to not want or need much from a material standpoint. Many times, these people are also quite happy. You may also know people who have a lot of money and possessions, but always want more. They never seem to BeHappy! with what they have.

It's just common sense that if your desires or expectations exceed your needs and financial resources, you will not be as happy as possible over the long term. I say *over the long-term* because as described above under the discussion of goals, these desires and needs, if leading you toward a better life, can create happiness by providing hope, motivation, and growth potential. It's the desire without the goals — or no clear plan to achieve those goals — that will prevent happiness. Also, if you consistently spend more money than you earn, you will end up creating significant stress and difficulty in your life. So, your lifestyle and expectations can be a significant factor in your overall happiness — especially if you are not wealthy or do not want to be rich.

The ability to manage this issue comes from maintaining a grounded sense of expectation while not compromising your goals and dreams. If, for example, you have a solid career, providing you an annual income of $100,000, it might be extreme to expect to buy a five million dollar home, a three million dollar yacht and two vacation cottages (unless, of course, you were already very wealthy through some other means). These purchases could be major goals for you, but it would require a plan to achieve those goals; like successfully investing a significant portion of your income for many years, creating a multi-million dollar net worth that would allow you to afford these types of luxuries. Simply wanting or expecting these things without the appropriate goals, plans, and financial resources would just lead to feelings of frustration and unhappiness.

Therefore, the bottom line is to learn to manage your expectations, while simultaneously using goals to take you to the levels of lifestyle and abundance you want. This can be easier said than done. Again, there are many personal development materials available to help achieve this. Use them.

STAY OUT OF DEBT

The more debt you assume, the more you must eventually pay up. In many cases, debt and happiness can be inversely related. Significant or excess debt can increase stress, inhibit freedom, and even break up relationships.

There is no question that some debt can be good, at the appropriate level and the right time. But you must have a plan and you must manage your finances. Maxing out credit cards and taking out multiple loans is a common path to disaster, creating significant stress and potentially destroying happiness.

I remember a time when I was in significant debt. Other than the death of my father and being in the wrong relationship at one point in my life, it was the most "unhappy" time in my life. It was extremely stressful and humiliating. I had to even sell my car at auction and go back living with my mother. I was 30 years old.

I got into this situation because I did not live within my means and got into more and more debt. Soon the IRS (who has very little flexibility and no sense of humor) came knocking. They forced me to create a plan, and it was no fun! After significant struggle and difficulty, I got myself out of debt and committed to never getting into that position again. To this day, I maintain a zero credit card balance and have no debt. The Peace-of-mind this provides is incredible (**NOTE:** *Peace-of-mind is part of my personal* **Definition of Happiness**).

So, as discussed in the previous section, manage your expectations consistent with your income. Live below your means so you can save and invest. Keep credit card debt to a minimum (preferably non-existent since interest charges on credit cards are nearly criminal). My guideline is to pay off all credit card balances every month, incurring no interest charges and ensuring that I spend less than I make, saving and investing a significant percentage of my income every month (*Note:* if you go back and review my list of things that have made me happy in the past, on page 40, one of the entries was "stayed debt-free" and one was "saved over 40% of our after-tax income"). I point this out as an example of how looking back and noticing what has made you happy in the past can help you create your Happiness Plan (see Chapter Three).

Another important factor regarding debt is this: when tough times come around (and they always do at some point in life) if you are free from debt, you may be able to manage the situation much more easily and with much less stress.

Low debt also has the added psychological benefit of increasing certainty (stability) and creating a general sense of comfort and well-being — all of which augment the potential for greater happiness.

APPRECIATE WHAT YOU HAVE (BE GRATEFUL)

If you look at the people around you, you can always find someone who has it tougher than you. All it takes is a trip to some of the poorer third-world countries to really feel and understand this. But you do not have to travel that far to grasp the concept of appreciating what you have.

It does take reflection, though; sometimes daily reflection. There is so much for which we can be grateful. You must reflect on the many great things in your life. Even if your life is extremely challenging right now, there are always many things that are great about life. And, as

THINGS YOU CAN APPRECIATE RIGHT NOW:

- ❑ Sunrises
- ❑ Sunsets
- ❑ Your children
- ❑ Your spouse
- ❑ Your friends
- ❑ Your health
- ❑ Your ability to contribute
- ❑ Small wins and successes
- ❑ Your job
- ❑ Your freedom to look for a new job
- ❑ The control you have over your life
- ❑ Your parents
- ❑ The town where you live
- ❑ Music
- ❑ The contributions you make
- ❑ Your special skill(s)
- ❑ The beauty of nature
- ❑ The beach
- ❑ Your country
- ❑ Your talents
- ❑ Your hobbies
- ❑ Your opportunities

mentioned previously, medical research has demonstrated that people who are consistently grateful live longer.

It may be difficult, but it is essential for maximum happiness to have a continual sense of gratitude. So take a few minutes right now to list everything in your life that you can appreciate today. At the very least, list the things you think you could appreciate. Look at the examples in the box on the previous page. Things you can appreciate right now in your life are:

•

•

•

•

If you wrote down at least five things you can appreciate now, you are probably feeling a bit better than you did before. There should be a subtle feeling of pleasure. You might even find yourself smiling.

This is just a start, though. Your *Happiness Plan* must include a mechanism by which you feel grateful regularly. So stay the course and we wil get there.

IF YOU ALREADY HAVE LOTS OF MONEY...

If you have sufficient financial wealth to allow you to do what you want, when you want, and you are still not completely happy, there are several possible reasons.

1. It could be that money, and the luxuries money can buy, are not part of your *Definition of Happiness*;

2. As stated many times, if other parts of your *Definition* are not being fulfilled, you will not be as happy as possible; and/or

3. Even if material possessions and financial success or peace of mind are part of your *definition*, there may be other significant issues causing you to be unhappy. Examples include not

having great *relationships* (which was discussed in Chapter Four) or having significant *regrets* (which will be discussed in Chapter Nine).

It is even possible that, regardless of the amount of money you have, you may be in significant debt (which is stressful) or you may not fully appreciate what you have and want more (see above for discussions on staying out of debt and appreciating what you have). If you can identify what is making you unhappy, you can begin to release the effects of these pressures by using the tools in this book. It all starts by knowing what happiness means for you.

Regardless of your situation, however, there will always be tough times. Dealing with these tough times in life is another key component of being as happy as possible over the long-term, which is the subject of the next chapter.

CHAPTER SUMMARY & KEY POINTS

1. Money can help make you happier if the things money can do for you are somehow part of your *Definition of Happiness*.

2. If you do not have an abundance of money, there are several things you can do to still BeHappy! Also, if you don't have much money and would like to have more, there are things you can do to become wealthy (beyond the scope of this book).

3. If you are already wealthy and still not happy, many of the other concepts in this book could be the cause, like poor relationships and significant regrets. Using the tools here can improve your life tremendously.

PART THREE

Reality

*Life is not fair. It is also very complicated. Life can be painful and traumatic. Happy people, even extremely happy people, deal with these realities well. We are all individuals with different personalities and different **rules**. We sometimes do things we later **regret**. The intent of this section, therefore, is to address these realities of life and help deal with them ahead of time so the unfair and complex world can be more balanced and simple. This concept, along with the foundation and essential elements in Parts One and Two can be major factors in achieving overall happiness.*

7

CHANGING YOUR RULES

OBJECTIVES OF THIS CHAPTER

- To understand how rules affect our lives and our happiness.

- Defining rules and what they mean to our relationships with others.

- How to eliminate some rules and change other rules into guidelines.

We all have "rules" which guide our opinions, decisions, and actions. Many times we don't realize we have these rules, but they are there. We start creating these rules early in life based on our upbringing, our learning process and our experiences. And while some rules are necessary, having too many rules creates tension and frustration. Also, since everyone's background and life experiences are different, we all create different rules, which leads to conflict. In fact, according to Tony Robbins, any upset between people is related to differing rules. And I believe this is true. Whether it is two people in an argument or two countries at war, generally the conflict is a result of a difference in rules.

The rules we create for ourselves during our life can lead to significant distress and, many times, outright unhappiness. And the

> "Any upset between people is always a 'rules' upset"
>
> — *Tony Robbins*

more rules you have, the more unhappiness you will experience. Therefore, as part of the journey towards greater happiness, this chapter deals with improving your life by altering, reducing, or even eliminating many of your rules.

Think about it — the more rules you have for how the world is supposed to be or how people are supposed to act, the more difficult it will be for those around you to live by those rules. And because they have different rules, people will surely "break your rules," which will make life all the more frustrating and difficult.

As a simple example, my wife Jill believes — because of her driven personality — that people should drive more aggressively, with purpose and assertiveness. This is one of her "rules." Not everyone has that same rule. In fact, many people have the completely opposite rule — that people should drive cautiously and not be in hurry or aggressive whatsoever. So as you can imagine, Jill often gets very frustrated while she is driving, especially where we lived recently — in Vancouver, British Columbia, Canada — a city with its fair share of slow, non-aggressive drivers (certainly when compared to a place like Southern California, where you'll find fast, aggressive drivers, all anxious to get somewhere). It's a whole different set of rules.

The only things Jill could do to reduce her frustration associated with this situation are:

1. Get everyone to become more aggressive drivers,

2. Make everyone change their rules,

3. Move back to Southern California, or

4. Change her own rule.

The first two are unlikely to happen. And, since we're not ready yet to move back to California, changing her own rule seems to be the best solution. Altering your rules is not easy, though. But if your mission is to BeHappy! changing your rules is a great way to improve the quality of your life by reducing stress, frustration, and conflict in your life. Here are four suggestions to help you manage this:

First, change as many of your RULES as possible to GUIDE-LINES. Doing this could have an immediate and profound effect on how you feel. In fact, many people experience an instantaneous sense of relief the moment something that used to be a rule is no longer quite as rigid. It is almost as if a huge weight was magically lifted from their shoulders and they seem to begin experiencing a better perspective on life.

Rules are rigid requirements, with distinct, narrow boundaries, which control the way life must be for you to BeHappy! *Guidelines, on the other hand, are flexible "guiding principles" with nebulous, wider boundaries that allow you to* BeHappy! *under a much broader range of circumstances.*

Second, as with many of the other tools mentioned in this book, it is important to identify what rules govern your life. Is it three or four rules or thirteen or fourteen, or even thirty or forty? The key is: the fewer the better. So whatever the number, reducing the rules that control your behavior and your attitude is a strategy that works. Reduce some of your rules (or make them more flexible by changing them to guidelines) and you will be happier. It's really that simple.

Take a look at the examples of some common rules which guide many people's lives (see the box on the next page). I'm sure you can see immediate sources of conflict and contradictions in some of these rules.

And what happens? If you live by some of these rules, every time someone breaks one of them, you experience negative emotions like anger, frustration, stress and/or anxiety. In fact, conflicting rules can cause couples to get divorced, long time friends to never speak again and nations to go to war.

Let's say, for example, you are married and one of your rules is that your spouse must have dinner on the table everyday when you get home from work. That's the way it was done in your family growing up and that's the way it must be now! It's your rule. So, what if you get home one evening after a stressful day at work, and there's no dinner being prepared? How do you feel? How do you react? What does it do to your evening? Generally it's not pleasant, right?

Even worse, what if that were your rule, but your spouse's rule was that the preparation of dinner in the evening was something that should be shared between a couple? Well, first off, the relationship would probably have gone nowhere — which is a problem in and of itself since some great relationships which were "meant to be" have ended unnecessarily due to differing rules. But if the relationship progressed to marriage, this rule conflict would tend to get more and more challenging, likely causing many fights and possibly even resulting in divorce — especially if there are several other "small" rules conflicts in the relationship.

The solution to this is simple, but difficult to achieve. Most people have some absolute rules they would never change or compromise. One example is the rule many couples have regarding monogamy. It is a very common and reasonable rule.

The objective here is not to suggest you consider lowering your standards or accepting things out-

COMMON RULES PEOPLE FOLLOW IN LIFE:

- ❑ My spouse must have dinner ready when I get home
- ❑ People must be more aggressive
- ❑ Children must be seen, not heard
- ❑ The toilet seat must always be put down after use
- ❑ Everything must be neat and tidy
- ❑ People must always be on time
- ❑ Abortion is murder
- ❑ Abortion is a choice
- ❑ My spouse must be "faithful"
- ❑ Polygamy is acceptable in marriage
- ❑ A friend is always there for you
- ❑ People must always be considerate
- ❑ People must be ambitious
- ❑ Work comes before family
- ❑ Family comes before work
- ❑ You can never have too many shoes
- ❑ Buying things on sale is being cheap
- ❑ Buying things on sale is smart

side your values, but rather to become *more flexible*, reduce your number of rules and create *guidelines* out of as many of your rules as possible.

To achieve this, think for a few minutes and spend some time writing down as many of your own rules as you can. As a starting point, if you have a spouse or significant other, think about what causes you to argue with that person most. Do the same with your family, friends and business associates — what causes you to argue with them? Use the list on the previous page to help you think of your rules. Write as many of your most important rules as you can here (be honest with yourself):

•

•

•

•

•

•

Hopefully you have very few rules. Like many people, however, you may have needed extra space to write them all down. If you have more than five major rules, the goal is to reduce the number to five or less. Also, the more that are "guidelines" instead of rules, the better. So, look through your list and either eliminate some you will no longer use as rules in your life or change them from a rule to a guideline, which in some cases can be done simply by changing words like "must," "never" or "always" to "should," "rarely" or "sometimes."

For example, if one of your rules is "people must always be on time," you can make this a guideline by changing it to "people should be on time as often as possible". Since people will not always be on time (many people have different rules about punctuality), you will frequently be frustrated and disappointed — especially if you keep the rule in its original form. By making it a

> *Key Point: Rules can create conflict, anxiety, pain, and disappointment, so you will be happier if you have fewer rules.*

guideline, some of the pressure will be lifted without compromising your own standards. In other words, it doesn't mean you will now be late. You just won't be as angry when you are the first to arrive somewhere.

Obviously, there are some rules which are more difficult to change than others. If you are married, you may not want to change anything about monogamy if that is your rule. That's fine — as long as your spouse has the same rule and it creates no conflicts.

Below are some examples of rules changed to guidelines. As you can see, in some cases this is accomplished simply by substituting *should* for *must*, or

RULE	GUIDELINE
Things must always be neat and organized	Things should be as organized as possible
Work is the number one priority	There should be balance between work & family
People must always be on time	Punctuality is a virtue
My spouse must always be faithful	Love conquers all
People must always return calls within 4 hours	People should return calls in a reasonable time
The toilet seat must be left down after use	Don't sweat the small stuff
•	•
•	•
•	•
•	•

always for *as much as possible*. Others are converted to guidelines by changing the complete focus of the rule. This usually has the greatest impact. Fill in the blanks in the box with some of your rules changed to guidelines.

Now that you've completed this task, go back through the entire list of *rules* you created earlier and change or eliminate as many as possible. Then begin to live by the new set of *guidelines* and see how you feel and how much more smoothly your life runs. But remember, it takes commitment to be successful. It also takes time. But it will be worth it since it will allow you to be happier. You must review these concepts regularly and get back on track when you deviate from the course. To finish this section, write your revised, reduced list of rules/guidelines here (or in Appendix 3):

•

•

•

•

•

OTHER PEOPLE'S RULES

As difficult as it may be to change or eliminate some of your own rules, it is even more difficult to change other people's rules. Since it is a waste of time to think that you could get everyone to change their rules — even the people closest to you, here are two more things to focus on to become happier in life using rules.

First, if you have a spouse or significant other, it is very important to know their rules. Write down in the spaces below your concept of their main rules.

•

•

•

Do they have lots of rules? Do many of their rules conflict with some of yours? If so, this is surely a source of disagreement and frustration.

The steps necessary to reduce the frustration and conflict are:

1. Know as much about their rules as possible and do what you can to avoid breaking them; and

2. Help them adjust or reduce their rules, just as you have now done, making some of them guidelines and eliminating others altogether. This requires communication.

Let's take this process a step further. The more you understand the rules of the people you spend your time with (family, friends and co-workers), the more you can help reduce the tension and frustration associated with their rules, and the happier your life will be. Again, since it is easier to change our own attitudes towards rules than theirs, much of the responsibility lies on each of us, since we cannot force others to change their rules. But just knowing other people's rules is of great benefit. And since our primary focus here is to BeHappy!, this is just one more tool to help you achieve the happiest life possible. Use it as much as you can, with as many people as you can, and your life will be much better for it.

To do this effectively, list on a sheet of paper the people you spend most of your time with — including friends, family members, co-workers, team members, business associates, etc. Once you have this list, write down the rules you know they have created or tend to follow in their lives. This alone will go a long way toward being less frustrated with these people and probably improve your relationship with them.

APPRECIATING DIVERSITY

Another factor associated with rules is the diversity of cultures, beliefs, personalities and backgrounds of people in our shrinking "global village." These cultural variations create significant differences in rules amongst people. Appreciating this diversity, instead of degrading those with different ethnic, religious or historically derived "rules" will reduce anxiety and frustration in your life. Learn to appreciate the diversity surrounding you as much as possible, even if you do not agree with the views and actions of people who are different from you.

In summary, rules and diversity are big sources of frustration and conflict in life. Reduce the number of your rules, or change some of them to guidelines, and you can **BeHappy!**

CHAPTER SUMMARY & KEY POINTS

1. Everyone has rules.

2. Differences in people's rules generally cause conflict.

3. The more rules you have, the harder it will be to be completely happy and the fewer your number of rules, the easier it will be to be completely happy.

4. Reducing your number of rules, and changing as many as possible to *guidelines*, is key to happiness.

5. Knowing the rules of the people you spend time with can help make you happier by having less conflict and frustration in your life.

8

DEALING WITH
THE TOUGH TIMES

OBJECTIVES OF THIS CHAPTER

- To understand that life always includes some tough times, challenges, problems, and pain.

- Developing ways to deal with these difficult times most effectively so you can still be happy, regardless of the circumstances.

- To learn from these tough times and even begin to cherish them.

AN INTRODUCTORY NOTE ABOUT THIS CHAPTER

I met my cousin, Jay, for the first time in around 1970, when I was 12. He was 17 at the time and was one of the most handsome, intelligent, physically fit guys I had ever met. He was perfect and I wanted to be just like him. His parents, my uncle Harry and aunt Georgia, were active, passionate, happy people. They were vibrant and "alive". They had a great life — with successful careers, an active social life, and a passion for tennis. They were so proud of Jay, their only son and their two daughters, Karen and Mauri.

A couple of years later, while driving home from work late one night, Jay fell asleep at the wheel of his car and was killed tragically in a terrible crash at the age of 19. As anyone can imagine, uncle Harry and aunt Georgia were devastated. Their life would never be the same. They became different people in my opinion. From then on, they appeared somewhat withdrawn and somber, with less passion and excitement for life. They even looked different to me. Uncle Harry, who had quit smoking years before, started smoking again. They even quit playing tennis. It would be understandable for them to never truly BeHappy! *again under these horrible circumstances.*

This chapter is about the harsh realities of everyday life — the "tough times". We all know life has them. But there are tough times — like financial difficulties and divorce — and there are <u>really</u> tough times — like the death of a spouse, or the unthinkable death of one of your children.

Many things in life are relative. Compared to the death of a child, everything else is relatively minor. So, in the context of the goals of this book, I do not want to imply that you should be totally happy if you were to experience something as brutally painful as the death of one of your children.

If you have experienced this type of trauma, the objective of this book is just to help you get through the next week, the next month, and the next year. It would not be expected for you to be as happy as you could be, especially in the short-term. But even under these circumstances, you can still have a better life. That's all that could be expected and my goal for anyone going through this type of "really tough time" would be to help in any way possible.

NOW, FOR A DISCUSSION OF THE "TOUGH TIMES" ...

Anyone who lives life to the fullest and takes risks is in danger of having things go wrong. It's just the way life is. Interestingly, however, according to many people, ultimate happiness and great achievements are only possible by going through some pain in the process.

It is very clear that life is not always fair, so when we are faced with problems, challenges and difficult circumstances — many of

> *"Any great achievement is preceded by many difficulties and lessons; great achievements are not possible without them."*
>
> *— Brian Tracy*

which are beyond our control — our ability to realize complete happiness may become somewhat blurred.

To deal with this fact in the context of a journey toward true happiness, you must first just accept this as a fact of life. There is no getting around it.

It is also important to keep in mind that difficult problems and hardships can also become agents for growth. Growing requires us to take risks, solve problems and manage failures. To help you appreciate how difficulties lead to happiness, here is a great commentary from Paul Harvey, the well-known journalist:

"We tried so hard to make things better for our kids that we made them worse.

For my grandchildren, I'd like better.

I'd really like for them to know about hand me down clothes and home-made ice cream and leftover meat loaf sandwiches. I really would. I hope you learn humility by being humiliated and that you learn honesty by being cheated. I hope you learn to make your own bed and mow the lawn and wash the car.

And I really hope nobody gives you a brand new car when you are sixteen.

It will be good if at least one time you can see puppies born and your old dog put to sleep.

I hope you get a black eye fighting for something you believe in. I hope you have to share a bedroom with your younger brother. And it's all right if you have to draw a line down the middle of the room, but when he wants to crawl under the covers with you because he's scared, I hope you let him.

When you want to see a movie and your little brother or sister wants to tag along, I hope you'll let him or her.

I hope you have to walk uphill to school with your friends and that you live in a town where you can do it safely.

On rainy days when you have to catch a ride, I hope you don't ask your driver to drop you two blocks away so you won't be seen riding with someone as uncool as your Mom.

If you want a slingshot, I hope your Dad teaches you how to make one instead of buying one.

I hope you learn to dig in the dirt and read books. When you learn to use computers, I hope you also learn to add and subtract in your head.

I hope you get teased by your friends when you have your first crush and when you talk back to your mother that you learn what ivory soap tastes like.

May you skin your knee climbing a mountain, burn your hand on a stove and stick your tongue on a frozen flagpole.

I don't care if you try a beer once, but I hope you don't like it. And if a friend offers you dope or a joint, I hope you realize he is not your friend.

I sure hope you make time to sit on a porch with your Grandma or Grandpa and go fishing with your Uncle.

May you feel sorrow at a funeral and joy during the holidays.

I hope your mother punishes you when you throw a baseball through your neighbor's window and that she hugs you and kisses you at Hanukkah/Christmas time when you give her a plaster mold of your hand.

These things I wish for you — tough times and disappointment, hard work and happiness.

To me, it's the only way to appreciate life."

Yes, the challenges, problems, and difficulties we face in life truly can help make us happier in the long run. Think about it. Hasn't overcoming some difficulty in your life made you a stronger person? And, hasn't that accomplishment and increased strength translated into better self-esteem and more self-confidence? The reason for this is that we are happiest when we are growing and learning.

There is no argument that people with high self-esteem are happier and healthier. Solving problems, dealing with challenges, and enduring pain help build self-esteem and self-confidence. While accepting these facts may make difficulties easier to manage, it will probably not eliminate negative emotions or pain.

Many self-help books advise us to "appreciate the tough times," mainly for the reasons I have mentioned. While this is true, it is certainly easier said than done. The tough times are not fun, but

> *"Difficulties come not to obstruct, but to instruct"*
>
> — *Brian Tracy*

by enduring them — and learning from them — you can be directed toward your ultimate happiness. The goal, therefore, is to be able to embrace tough times with courage, hope and expectation. Here are 3 steps to achieving that objective:

Preparation — In other words, be prepared — reduce your chances of being surprised or caught off guard. Tough times, disappointments and pain are part of life. Being prepared for them can definitely make them easier to handle.

Management — When going through a tough time, manage it in the most efficient, practical way possible. This will help ease the pain and get you through tough times more smoothly.

Reflection — We are happiest when we are growing. Keep in mind that learning from tough times means growth, which further prepares you for the next time a similar situation comes around.

Let's address each of these points separately.

PREPARATION

Adversity starts as soon as we are born. Paul Harvey's commentary focuses on how difficulties and disappointments can prepare us to be more appreciative of life. Some of the most traumatic moments in my own life (the early death of my father, a failed relationship which ended in divorce, the death of a good friend, and financial difficulties) have done a lot to prepare me for many of life's current and future tough times. I am very confident now — because of these challenges in my own life — in my ability to deal with these types of hardships.

In addition, I've found that preparation can also involve some proactive strategies. For example, many of life's most painful moments can involve financial struggles. As mentioned in Chapter Six, you can be better prepared for these types of issues by staying out of debt and putting aside some funds into an emergency account to be used only in the case of a crisis.

Adequate health insurance is also important in helping to deal with the sudden burden a serious illness or disease can impose on your finances. In addition, the better understanding you have of the main health issues facing people today can help avoid many health problems or at least prepare you to better deal with a medical condition you may encounter.

Being prepared for potential challenges in your career (e.g., "you're fired") might include making sure that you continue to develop your technical or professional skills so as to remain in high demand for another job.

You can also be better prepared by having multiple streams of income, which should be part of everyone's financial strategy. This can be achieved by making investments in different companies, doing work outside your normal job, gaining additional talents and skills, making a hobby an income-producing activity, and more.

Again, having enough money set aside helps to more easily get through some of the financial difficulties we may face.

Of course, there is no way to prepare for all of life's challenges. And this book cannot attempt to address the countless types of problems and difficulties any one of us might have to face throughout our life. The objective here, therefore, is to recognize that preparation will help ease the pain of life's tough times. It is up to you to identify what your anticipated challenges might be and then find the best way to prepare for them. This will be done later as part of your *Happiness Plan*.

MANAGEMENT

Preparation can only go so far primarily because, as stated previously, you cannot anticipate nor expect to prepare for every conceivable difficult situation or adversity. But, when hard times do occur, you must also be prepared to go into a crisis management mode to handle the situation in the best way possible. Obviously the more prepared you are, the better you will manage the process.

There are also several steps you can take to get through many tough situations more effectively and with the least amount of pain possible. These are:

1. **MAINTAIN PERSPECTIVE** — Put the situation into proper perspective.

2. **ANALYZE THE SITUATION** — Define the issue(s).

3. **PLAN** — Create a plan to address the issue(s).

4. **LEARN** — Remember there is something good about every situation. Learn from it.

Many times, just completing the first two steps above — maintaining perspective and analyzing the situation — will help reduce the emotional part of the problem or difficulty significantly. I don't know how, it just does. Let me explain.

When faced with a crisis or difficult problem, as most people, I feel an uncomfortable, nagging feeling inside that sometimes will not subside. But just by putting the situation into perspective and defining the issue clearly, I immediately feel much more at ease and can function much better. It seems to break a "big problem" into several smaller, more manageable pieces. This then helps me create a more effective plan to resolve the issues.

Creating an effective plan requires sharp analysis and a definition of each of the issues involved in the problem or situation. Once each component of a problem or difficult situation is defined and identified for what it really is, a simpler plan can be created to address each issue. This is much more productive than the initial emotional response we most often mount.

At a minimum, this will put the problem into better perspective and hopefully make the situation less daunting. Following through with the plan will then lead to an organized, calmer approach to resolving the problem — hopefully forever.

Finally, keeping in mind that it is possible to find something good about every situation — regardless of how bad it may seem at the time — is critically important. Our disposition or attitude about life and our own individual situation plays a big role in our ability to BeHappy! regardless of the circumstances. By searching for the good in any negative situation and focusing on the positive, you will be able to better handle any consequences associated with the issues. So, when faced with a challenge in life, ask yourself the question: "What's good about this?" Then force yourself to come up with some useful, empowering answers. Look hard. They always exist.

REFLECTION

Once a negative situation has been resolved, or just subsides, reflect on the situation and its resolution. This will help in many ways. We can learn from every experience — especially the negative ones.

First, by learning from the experience, you are better prepared for the next similar challenge. Also, you will gain more confidence, which will help you deal with difficult circumstances more effectively. Often reflection also creates more motivation and opportunity.

A great example is seven-time *Tour de France* champion, Lance Armstrong. As mentioned earlier, he went through one of the most difficult of life's challenges — a diagnosis of cancer and the associated treatment. Although he may not have been prepared for this unexpected challenge, he managed it well and reflected upon his experience, adding a whole new purpose to his life in the process — helping others with cancer manage their situation. In addition, from a motivational perspective, he says he never would have won seven straight *Tour de France* cycling races if he had not gone through the experience (he won all seven after beating cancer). The experience created an intense motivation in him to live life to the fullest, be the best he could be, and lead a more "purpose-filled" life. What he learned from the experience has been invaluable. He has probably become happier and more fulfilled as a result.

So, preparation, management and reflection are three steps to take in helping deal with the tough times of life. The more effectively you are able to utilize each of these in your life, the happier you will become, regardless of the circumstances.

In addition to these three steps, there is another fundamental concept critical to happiness in life. It's called...Enjoying the Process.

ENJOYING THE PROCESS

A wonderful book by Dan Milman, *The Peaceful Warrior*, emphasizes the importance of "living in the moment" and "enjoying the process" as part of your personal development toward a happy life.

Essentially his message is to live for today and, except for the **happy** times you've experienced (which was discussed in Chapter Three), do not dwell on the past nor wait for something to occur in the future to be happy. He also urges people to enjoy the "process" (of life), even if the process will be, at times, almost unbearably painful.

To emphasize the point with a rather extreme example of "living in the moment" and "enjoying the process", Millman invites us to picture ourselves falling from a tall building, suggesting that "someone living truly in the moment would enjoy the trip down!"

Surely for most of us, this philosophy would be difficult to comprehend as being enjoyable. But it certainly makes the point. It would require you to give up thinking about the future and dwell on nothing negative from the past, but rather to enjoy the view and appreciate everything you have done in your life as you are heading toward the ground.

No one reading this book is in as bad a situation as someone falling from a skyscraper — regardless of how tough your life may seem right now. But life can be tough and full of pressures, like financial crises, problems with spouses or children, and health issues. Most of us have to work hard for a living and most people don't really *love* their job. So, how can we "enjoy the process" in spite of all of this? There are many answers to this question.

First, make certain you are living consistent with your identity and consider defining your mission or *purpose* if you have not already done so. We touched on this in Chapter Two, and while we did not go into fully defining your purpose or your mission, it is something you should do as part of this to journey to finding complete and total happiness. (The book, *Becoming Real*, by David Irvine has a great description of how to design your personal mission statement.)

Second, begin making a concerted effort to appreciate — even relish — problems and difficulties, viewing them as much as possible as challenges and opportunities to grow by proving to yourself how great you are at dealing with adversity. In fact, if you can, as much as possible, think of it as a game. Even a crisis situation can often be made enjoyable, at least in hindsight.

Third, as stated, never forget to appreciate what you do have right now. The more you are able to do this, the easier any tough situation you have to face will become. (If you need more ideas about what you can appreciate in your life, there is a great little book by Barbara Ann Kipfer called *14,000 Things to be Happy About*.)

Finally, strive to *live in the moment* rather than dwell on the past or worry about the future. To do this requires you to:

— Always keep the *Big Picture* in mind.
— Know your purpose in life — your mission — and live by it.
— Understand that challenge and failure are growth opportunities.
— Make the challenges of life a game — have fun.
— Appreciate what is great about your life right now — in the present.
— Maintain an optimistic attitude.
— Live consistent with your identity.

A personal example of focusing on the big picture, living consistent with your identity and having a purpose:

My current career is very stressful. I am the Chief Executive Officer of a publicly traded biotech company in Vancouver on the west coast of Canada. So first, being from the United States, my wife and I have been living in a foreign country (while it's not China, India or Afghanistan, Canada is still different in many ways from the US). Second, biotechnology and the business of drug development, is an extremely high-risk, intense and competitive business.

Most biotech companies fail and there is a constant need for raising cash. The majority of biotech companies have little or no revenues for long periods of time. There is lots of speculative money at stake, very complex science, and a difficult, lengthy FDA drug-approval process. On top of all this, the investors (shareholders), anxiously hoping for a big win, are extremely demanding. The process of discovering, researching and developing a drug takes a decade on average and only one out of every ten thousand compounds ever makes it into the marketplace.

If I were to think about the details of all this on a regular basis, I'm not sure I could ever love what I am doing, even though I thrive on the challenge of it all. Instead, I keep focused on the bigger picture, which, in our case is the company's mission — to improve people's lives. Therefore, just the thought of getting one drug to market is tremendously empowering and motivating. Keeping this mission in mind provides the fundamental foundation for why (and how) my team and I can enjoy something that, on a day-to-day basis, is extremely stressful and complex.

But even that may not be enough. Fundamentally, what helps me enjoy and even love our mission is the fact that it is fulfills my personal and professional commitment to improve people's lives. So I am also living consistent with my identity and my purpose in life is being fulfilled.

Let me contrast this with my previous career as a practicing physician. Like my current career it was also very stressful and intensely demanding and I was also in the business of improving people's lives. It was very rewarding from that perspective since I was again fulfilling my purpose. But, ultimately I was not as happy as I could be since there were too many other aspects of medical practice which did not fit as well with my identity. As a creative person with strengths in leadership, vision and strategy, I was not utilizing my true talents fully in medical practice.

How does this relate to you? It relates perfectly if you are not enjoying your life. If you go through the process the way I described it in the example of my job above, you can live consistent with your identity, love what you do, and be much, much happier.

* * * *

To conclude this chapter, let me relay a story told to me by my friend, Eve, in Vancouver. One of her best friends growing up had a skiing accident just before his 20th birthday, leaving him paralyzed from the neck down. For a while after the accident, he went through some very difficult times, driv-

> *"I am still determined to be cheerful and happy, in whatever situation I may be; for I have also learned that the greater part of our happiness depends upon our dispositions, and not upon our circumstances."*
>
> — *Martha Washington*
> *(1732-1802)*

ing him to hunger strikes, ill temper and periods of rage and a lack of any direction in his life. Within a couple of years to alcoholism and creating other significant health issues. But he pulled himself out of this situation, turned his life around, went back to school, got his MBA and is now a successful business leader. This is a normal person who achieved extraordinary results after incredible life difficulties and challenges (much greater challenges than most of us face). He eventually managed his tough times, started living in the moment, created positive expectations for the future, and is a happy, fulfilled person today.[7]

Surely, most of us have been fortunate enough not to have faced this kind of difficulty and challenge in our lives. Most of us let "the little things" get us down. We are bothered by the amount of taxes we might have to pay or even the loss of a job — which is surely a tough matter. But these issues are nowhere near as tough as losing the normal use of most of your body for the rest of your life.

So, strive to create a disposition that allows you to be happy regardless of your circumstances. Develop an attitude of gratitude. There are always things in our lives for which we can be grateful. *Prepare* for the tough times in your life so that you can *manage* them well. *Reflect* on what you can learn from every challenge you endure. Then, live in the moment and BeHappy! as you go through the ups and downs of life. It will make a huge difference.

CHAPTER SUMMARY & KEY POINTS

1. Tough times are a part of life, so an ability to deal with these tough times when they come along is a key component of happiness.

2. There are things you can do to prepare for life's difficult times.

3. When the tough times occur, reflect and learn from them.

4. Living in the moment with an ability to enjoy the process are effective ways to get through tough times, especially when they are prolonged.

5. Your overall attitude or disposition can determine your level of happiness under many different kinds of circumstances.

9

REGRETS

OBJECTIVES OF THIS CHAPTER

- To decrease the chances you will have major regrets in your life.
- Develop an understanding of how regrets negatively affect your life and your ability to be completely happy.
- To reduce or eliminate the effects of the regrets you already have.

DO YOU HAVE ANY *REGRETS* in your life? Do you regret doing something or not having done something? Most people do. Some are small regrets. Some are large. But either way, the *regrets* we have can strip us of some degree of happiness.

To be as happy as possible, it is vital to acknowledge the regrets you already have. You should also recognize and understand that there will be regrets in the future — primarily so you can use this knowledge to minimize the number and impact of those regrets.

An effective way to address this and make yourself happier is through a process called the "*rocking chair test.*" Maybe you have heard of it. It is where you picture yourself at a very old age, sitting in your "rocking chair," thinking back on your life. You picture yourself sitting there, reflecting on what was great and what was not so great about your time here on this earth.

If you were to do that right now, what result would you get? Would it be mostly positive? If there are negatives, it could be due to certain *regrets* you have about your life. If it is mostly negative, the reason could be the result of some major *regrets* you have, or even the accumulation of a large number of smaller regrets. The more *regrets* you have in life, and the larger the magnitude of those *regrets*, the less happy you will be as you grow older. That's why a whole chapter is devoted to the subject.

So what regrets would you have as you take this *rocking chair test*? Not going to college or having children? If so, these are relatively major events — things that would have changed your entire life. Would you regret something relatively small, like missing your twentieth high school reunion or a friend's wedding?

Think about it right now. What could you possibly do in your life that you might eventually regret having done? Is it cheating on your taxes or on your spouse? What about stealing something from someone, betraying the trust of a friend, or doing "recreational drugs?" If you can think of similar answers to this question, these are the types of things you must absolutely avoid doing in the future.

By the same token, you should also ask yourself, "what have I *not* yet done that I might regret not having done later?" Is it learning a second language? What about going to college, learning a new trade or skill, or becoming a guitar player? Is it not having children or spending more time with the children you have? If any of these types of things could apply to you, it is critical that you do something now to avoid developing some major regrets later.

> *Key Point: Regrets can destroy happiness. The more regrets you have in life, the less happy you will be. As you progress through life, the more regrets are accumulated, the more unhappy you will be late in life. The "rocking chair test" is a great way to anticipate potential regrets before they occur and even resolve regrets you may already have.*

Deep regrets can erode happiness — perhaps destroy it completely — if they are big enough. Even several small regrets can add up to be detrimental to your happiness. Fortunately, there are techniques we can use today to reduce their effect on our ultimate happiness tomorrow.

An Example of How Regrets Could Affect Your Happiness Forever…

I mentioned earlier my father died unexpectedly while I was in medical school. This was one of my life's most difficult, painful times.

During that week when he became ill, I felt helpless and afraid. After five days of continued deterioration in his condition, the doctors treating him began preparing us for the worst. I couldn't believe it! The possibility that my father, only 57 years old, could die was unthinkable. He was healthy just a week before.

Being in medical school I felt there must be something I could do. That is when Dr. Roy Behnke crossed my mind. Dr. Behnke was "the doctor's doctor". He was the ultimate physician. The med students called him "a god". If Dr. Behnke could not save my father's life, nobody could.

I will never forget it. It was late on a Sunday night and we were all desperate. The doctors had now told us my father would not survive. I had to do something. But surely I could not disturb Dr. Behnke, this important physician, at home late on a Sunday night. But that's exactly what I did. I didn't even know how to contact him at first. His number was unlisted. But this was my father's life at stake. Nothing is impossible. I found a way to contact him through a neighbor, a family member, and another professor at the university.

I hesitantly called Dr. Behnke, introduced myself as one of his students (I'm sure he didn't put my name with my face on the phone) and explained the situation to him. Another challenge was that Dr. Behnke did not even have "privileges", as they are called, at the hospital where my father was being treated. Privileges at a specific hospital are required before a physician can perform any services at that hospital. It is a long, bureaucratic, legal process. Again, we found a way to get him immediate "courtesy" privileges that Sunday night.

Dr. Behnke arrived about an hour later and I felt an immediate sense of relief. After examining my father for over two hours (it was past midnight) he sat down with me and told me things did not look good. He was adding to my father's treatment and doing some things the other doctors had not considered, but it was still a long shot.

My father died about two days later, so the outcome was no different, even with Dr. Behnke's input. The point here, however, is that I have no regrets about the situation. Think of how I would have felt, perhaps for the rest of my life, if I had decided to not "disturb" Dr. Behnke at his home late on that Sunday night. I would have always thought there was more we could have done and that my father might even be alive today if I had just made that call. What a burden that would have been. I would have regretted it forever. I might have even felt partially responsible for my father's death and surely, total happiness may never have been possible for me with that regret. As it stands, even though I still feel the pain and miss my father daily, I have no regrets and feel great about what we did. I also will be eternally grateful to Dr. Roy Behnke, at the USF College of Medicine, for being there with us to help.

* * * *

As one final exercise, it is important to take the rocking chair test right now. Here's how: look ahead to the future — many years from now and imagine yourself somewhere between 70 and 90 years old. You have lived most of your life and there is little you can do to change what you have done and limited time to address what you have not done.

Is there anything you have *done*, looking back on your life, that you regret? What have you *not done* that you regret not doing? We will divide this exercise into two parts — the first part includes what you have already done, as of today, which you regret. The second is to list what you might regret if you did it, but have not yet done. So to begin, use the space provided to answer this question:

What have you done already (as of today) you regret?

•

•

•

•

Now that you have this information (you have taken the time to do the exercise, right?), it is important to take action. Here's how: look at your list — the things you regret having done already. Are there any? If not, you are lucky. If so, there is obviously nothing you can do to turn back the clock. There are two things you can do, however, to make the situation better and reduce, or even eliminate, the regret you feel.

First, you can commit to never doing these types of things again. While that sounds simple and obvious, it is not always easy to achieve. If you are a smoker, for example, and regret having started, it may very a very difficult habit to eliminate. Perhaps even more difficult is the second thing you can do, which is something to counteract or buffer the effects of the things you regret.

In other words, you can create a feeling so positive from the experience you regret that you can actually come to appreciate the experience. Following through with the example above, if you regret having smoked cigarettes, or even

COMMON THINGS PEOPLE REGRET DOING

- Stealing
- Doing drugs
- Having an extramarital affair
- Not eating healthy
- Smoking
- Spending too much time at work
- Spending too much money (not saving)
- Wasting too much time
- Losing a friend over something trivial
- Getting pregnant too young
- Waiting too long to have children
- Staying in a bad relationship

doing drugs at some point in your life, you might decide to help children never start smoking or addicts get off drugs — or do whatever you can to educate others so they never start. You could volunteer to speak about the negatives of drugs and cigarettes at elementary schools or perhaps just be a steady force of positive reinforcement about these issues with friends, family or other people over which you have some degree of influence.

But…you must do something proactive. And by doing this, by sharing your experience, you could be a huge contributing factor by helping people avoid making the same mistakes — perhaps even save someone's life.

The intensely positive feeling you will receive by virtue of this contribution will help counterbalance and possibly even entirely eliminate your feeling of regret. Depending on how positive the feeling is, you may even be grateful for the lessons learned and character created within you by the very thing you used to regret.

Even if your regret involves something you did to a friend or family member no longer living, you may still be able to make things better. It's up to you to be creative and figure out how. As crazy as it may sound, one idea involves writing a letter to this person even though you "know" they will never get the message. Or will they? Maybe you could do something special for someone that was close to that person to contribute to their life in some meaningful way. At the very least, the therapeutic value of getting it "out of your system" and making a contribution to someone will make you feel much better.

These actions may not prove to be a total substitute for the regret you might feel. There are surely many things that cannot be undone completely. That's life! But it is possible to reduce the negative effects it has on your future happiness.

Now, for the second part of this process. What have **you not** done yet…but might be capable of doing later in your life which you might regret? Stealing something? Hurting someone? Taking advantage of others? Cheating?

Write your response to that question here:

-
-
-
-
-

Identifying the things you *could* regret may be much more difficult than identifying those actions you already regret. This involves both looking into the future as well as being **very** honest with yourself — and you may have trouble with either of those two challenges. So think hard about what are you capable of doing in your life that you would regret? What have been your capabilities in the past? This could help you identify what you could do in the future.

This is a very important list for you at this point, because once you have it the way you want it, you must review it regularly — at least once a year (more often if possible). Keep it in a place where you can review and recommit on a regular basis to never doing. Doing this could help avoid the pain of many regrets in the future, perhaps some major ones, which will have a profound effect on your ability to **BeHappy!**

You now have two lists of things which you either already regret having done, or which you could see yourself possibly doing and regretting later in your life.

The next question to answer as you sit in your imaginary rocking chair is: "What is it that I have not yet done in my life that I will regret not having done?" Write your answer to this question in the spaces below.

What have you not done that you will regret not having done in your life?

•

•

•

•

•

Was it not going to college or never having children? What about not working toward becoming a professional athlete? Could it be not taking a year off from your job, living on a boat and traveling the South Sea Islands or working a season at a ski resort in Switzerland? Could it be not spending more time with your family or simply not giving your spouse more love and affection? What about not taking certain risks or building more adventure into your life? Also, look at your list of standards/values in Chapter Two. Not

COMMON THINGS PEOPLE REGRET NOT DOING IN THEIR LIVES

- "Being there" for their kids
- Pursuing a certain career
- Finishing school
- Eating more healthy
- Exercising regularly
- Quitting smoking
- Spending more time with family
- Keeping in touch with friends
- Learning another language
- Learning to play a musical instrument
- Seeking more adventure in life
- Working less
- Saving more money
- Pursuing a particular relationship
- Making certain investments
- Traveling more (seeing the world)
- Communicating better with a loved one
- Living in a different country
- Living on a boat for a while
- Asking a certain person out on a date
- Being more adventurous
- Believing in a higher power

living up to those standards could be a start.

Depending on your own personal situation, some of these things may no longer be feasible. If you are a woman over fifty, for example, and you regret never having children, it may be difficult or too risky to bear a child. If you regret not becoming a professional basketball player in the NBA, but stand five feet tall, it may be a very difficult goal to achieve. But you could find substitutes that might reduce the regret you feel.

While some things may not be realistic at this point, you can create viable substitutes. And, believe it or not, there are many issues you may have written down that can be changed. There is nearly always time to do something about it.

If you really believe you will always regret never going to college, for example, it is **never** too late. I've heard of people going back to school in their 80's and even 90's. If you would regret, while sitting in that rocking chair, that you never pursued a career in photography, make it your next goal — at least as a hobby. By being creative, you can either achieve exactly what you want, or produce a practical substitute that will make a positive difference as you sit in your rocking chair many years from now.

If, for example, you regret not having children in your life, you should consider seriously making sure it is part of your plan. But it could be too late to bear a child (depending on your age and circumstances). You could, however, volunteer at a Children's Home or even adopt a child (a much bigger responsibility).

As another example, if you are a great athlete and think you might regret not participating in serious competitive sports, there are many opportunities to do so, for people of all ages. It may not be the "Pros," but the feeling you would get could be just as profound. Like most things, the key is to make a commitment and take action. It is totally up to you. So *JUST DO IT!*

Look at Victoria Jackson — a grandmother from Winnipeg, Manitoba, Canada — who was the first woman to kayak the Northwest Passage starting in the summer of 1991 and completing her odyssey alone in 1994. While it wasn't Olympic competition, it was probably an even prouder (happier) moment for her to accomplish such a tremendous goal at her age.

Action Plan To Eliminate Regrets from your Life: Take some time now and generate a list of things you will do — actions you will take — over the next few days, weeks, months, even years which could minimize any regrets you might have later in life. Use the most significant regrets and potential regrets you listed earlier and use the space below, Appendix 3, or a separate sheet of paper if you need more room to write:

Regret   **Action**

•   •

•   •

•   •

•   •

Use these action items to reduce or eliminate the regrets you already have or could have in your life. Life is a journey. Being as happy as you can be is its own journey. The course will certainly be challenging at times, but by using the right tools, being prepared for adversity, and making sure you have minimal regrets when you are sitting in your rocking chair near the end of your life, the journey can be spectacular. The fewer regrets in your life, the more positive your rocking chair test result will be. You'll have a big smile on your face and a warm feeling in your heart. You will BeHappy!

CHAPTER SUMMARY & KEY POINTS

1. Regrets, especially major ones, can destroy happiness.

2. There are things you can do to minimize or even eliminate the regrets you already have in your life.

3. Thinking ahead to regrets you could experience is one way to avoid them. The Rocking Chair Test is one technique to use to avoid regrets.

4. Happiness can be hindered by doing things you regret doing AND by NOT doing things you regret not doing.

PART FOUR

Creating Your " Happiness Plan"

*With the information you now possess, it is time to create the roadmap to your ultimate destination. This will be your personal **Happiness Plan**. Before devising the detailed plan, however, there are a few extra tools to help you create the best plan possible. Read on and then create the Plan that will lead you to lifelong happiness!*

10

SOME EXTRA TOOLS

TAKE PICTURES

"A picture is worth a thousand words." Pictures are also worth a thousand opportunities to BeHappy! They can provide daily chances to increase happiness, joy, and fulfillment in life by reminding us about what is important, what is positive, and what is possible in our lives.

I am a very visual person. While documenting my weekly and yearly activities, events and accomplishments, I found that by taking lots of pictures, I was able to better remember where I was and what I did during each year. Also, while reviewing these pictures throughout the year, new feelings of joy, fulfillment, gratitude, and excitement would be evoked — much like when I was actually there in the moment. Even when I was having a tough, stressful day, these pictures brightened my outlook. It was amazing. It took me right back into the moment; like being on our boat at Catalina Island, motivating a group of people at a business presentation, skiing at Whistler, or even Jill and me lounging on the couch watching a movie with our dog Sunny at our feet.

Every picture created positive emotions, making me laugh and sometimes even cry. It provided an added sense of gratitude so critical for being completely happy.

> "A picture is worth a thousand opportunities to create happiness"
>
> — *Jimmy DeMesa, MD*

That is why I have shared many pictures with you throughout this book. They are intended to accomplish three things: (1) give you ideas about activities or events you may want to include in your life, (2) provide examples for you of the types of pictures you should include in your monthly and yearly review, and (3) motivate you to experience all that life has to offer.

Skiing in Whistler, Canada.

I now take lots of pictures, thanks to my wife Jill, who convinced me to spend the money on a digital camera, partly so she could e-mail pictures to our family in Florida.

Once I had a digital camera, as I did my regular "year in review" process (which you will learn more about in the final chapter of the book), I began reviewing the pictures we took during those activities.

I have found that reviewing these special moments is a great technique for keeping joy and appreciation right in front of me constantly. Like everything though, it takes conscious effort, focus and commitment to actively make this a BeHappy! tool. Ultimately, it really must become a habit or part of your regular routine. And, it is important to use pictures that create positive memories and emotions.

As you employ these tools and go through the process of becoming truly happy, you can also accelerate and solidify your long-term emotions by doc-

umenting your activities, both in writing and with pictures. It's so very easy to do with the technology available today (and Jill's suggestion actually saved us lots of money since there are no film development costs associated with digital cameras). And it's fun at the same time.

If you haven't gone "digital" yet, you can start by buying an inexpensive digital camera. Then, assuming you have a computer, you can learn to download your pictures onto your computer so you have easy access to them — and within a short time you'll have paid for the camera with the money you save on film.

For cell phone users, another strategy might be to get a phone with a built-in camera (they are fairly standard these days). Although usually not the best quality pictures, this eliminates the need for you to remember your camera everywhere you go since you'll already have it with you. Keep in mind that the quality is not as important in these happy moment snapshots... since they are not generally meant to be printed or enlarged.

I download these pictures onto my computers, both at home and at the office, create CD's of the pictures, and review them regularly or sometimes even set up a "rolling" screensaver with many of these pictures — giving me continuous reminders and providing regular smiles. Try it. See if it helps you to BeHappy!

BE A "TEAM PLAYER"

One great tool to help enhance your happiness is to become part of a team and be a "team player". Let me explain.

In this context, a team is any group of people — typically two to fifteen — who have a common goal and a frequent, regular process toward achieving that goal.

There are all kinds of "teams" in life. It doesn't have to be a sports team or even some type of competitive situation, although competition helps strengthen the bonds of a team.

If you think about some of the happiest people you know, you'll probably find that most of them belong to some type of team — or at the very least were part of a strong team at one time. Try this: think back to a time in your life and recall what it was like when you were part of a team. It might have been a Little League baseball team or a volleyball team, a sewing club, a cheer leading squad or a church choir — anything that involved several people, with a common goal and regular interaction. It may have been many years ago, or it may be something you are actively involved in right now. It doesn't matter. Just think about the team.

Most people who do this get a smile on their faces as they remember the feelings that being a member of a team provided. People often have some of the most happy and fulfilling experiences of their lives when they were part of a team, especially if the team was successful and if growth and progress were involved.

This phenomenon regarding being part of a team (and being a team player) addresses many of the points in this book simultaneously. It helps establish new and better *relationships*. It can provide a sense of *purpose* and short-term goals. Depending on the type of team, it could even improve your *health* and fitness level if it involves physical activity. A team like an investment club could strengthen your financial situation. Other types of teams could provide entertainment and reduce stress. It is incredible what being part

EXAMPLES OF TEAMS

- ❑ Neighborhood softball league
- ❑ Church singing group
- ❑ Chess league
- ❑ Cooking group
- ❑ Hockey or soccer league
- ❑ Card players group
- ❑ Investment club
- ❑ Model car racing team
- ❑ A walking group
- ❑ A volunteer organization
- ❑ Pet walking team
- ❑ Fishing squad
- ❑ Musical group or band
- ❑ A women's or men's club
- ❑ Racquetball or squash club
- ❑ A shopping group
- ❑ Running club
- ❑ A bowling league
- ❑ Your work group
- ❑ A masterminding group
- ❑ Your company
- ❑ Yoga or Pilates class
- ❑ Any sports team
- ❑ A "breakfast club"
- ❑ Your family

of a team can add to your life by playing an important role in creating long-term happiness.

If you already participate on some type of team, great — then you probably know exactly what I'm talking about. If you are not currently part of a team, then join one or even start one. It could become a valuable part of your life.

But being on a team is only part of the experience. The other part is being a team player; because if you are on a team, but are out for the individual recognition or achievement, it is much less fulfilling.

Being a team player can actually lead to greater overall success in life. That's a bold statement, but it's true. The direct and indirect effects true teamwork creates can have far-reaching benefits beyond the team itself. So if success is something you value, as part of your path to happiness, being a team player will help get you there.

So be part of a team. Even more importantly, be a team player. It requires you to work toward something more than just yourself. It requires *contribution*. What this really means is an ability and desire to take care of the people on your team.

I experienced this first-hand when Neil Cantor and Sanford Mahr invited me to join their Mastermind Group in Tampa in 1995. What a team we became. We met every month, typically over dinner, and talked. We discussed life, relationships, success, wealth, happiness, and sadness. We created exercises for ourselves, which eventually "planted the seed" for my concept of this book series. It was a wonderful experience. In fact, I attended Neil's 75th birthday celebration recently and the memories we shared about those times together was another great source of happiness for all of us.

And really, when you think about it, we are all on many teams in life. We're on the team called our family. We are on a team if we work for a company. The people in the city where we live are part of *our team*.

Our Masterminding Group (What a team!)

While these are not the types of teams I discussed before, they are important *relationships*, and we must take care of them (as described in Chapter Four). Take care of the people on your team and you will be happier and more successful. Be creative. Be part of a team and be a team player. It will add to your happiness immensely.

INCLUDE A PET IN YOUR LIFE

Some people are "dog people" and some people are "cat people." Some people are "bird lovers." Some people don't like animals at all.

For most of my life I was never much of a "pet person." My wife Jill, on the other hand is — big time. So, guess what — we've had a pet since we were dating and all I can tell you is that I now would not want to be without one. It's such a source of joy and happiness.

For Jill and me, it's a golden retriever. We've had two retrievers. The first one was named Stoley and our current one is Sunny. They have both been wonderful additions to our lives.

Stoley was beautiful, smart and loving. Unfortunately, he died of cancer at the age of seven. Even with the pain of that situation, we never regret having him. He was an awesome dog and a huge source of happiness for us. And the memories stay with us today, several years later (he is on many of the pictures on our screensaver and in our homes).

Studies have shown that elderly people who own pets live longer and are happier, and more fulfilled. I believe this goes for people of all ages — even children suffering from cancer are happier when a dog is brought into their hospital room.

Jill, and our 3-year old golden retriever, Sunny, volunteer every week at hospitals — visiting sick and critically ill children. It's amazing how they respond. Children in severe pain — even in a coma — most of the time have a positive emotional response to the presence of a

Sunny as a puppy in Vancouver.

dog. They smile, laugh, and seemingly "forget" about their illness or injury for a few minutes.

One mother whose young daughter was in a coma told my wife that during her visit with Sunny, her daughter moved her hand and responded for the first time in weeks. It was great for Jill to just see how much hope this provided to the family. This can be the power of a pet.

But pets are definitely not for everyone. For those who can open their minds to this, however, it may be something to consider as another happiness tool. They certainly become part of your life and your family (part of your team), giving unconditional love and providing a source for giving it back.

They create fulfillment and joy and can help improve your social life. With a dog for example, you will also have something new in common to share and communicate about with many more people. It's great. We have a whole new group of friends, like Stephane and Fiona in Vancouver, whom we would probably have never met if we didn't have Sunny. And, their friendship is a whole new source off fun and fulfillment for Jill and I, not to mention a new best friend for Sunny — Stephane and Fiona's dog, Max.

LISTEN TO MUSIC...IT IS THE SOUNDTRACK OF LIFE

Could you imagine watching a movie without any of the background music or soundtrack? As important as the spoken words are to the content of the movie, music enhances the experience by adding excitement, drama, humor, or tension. Without it, a movie is basically dull and "lifeless." Just think how the shark scenes in the movie *Jaws* would have changed if the famous pounding music was not there.

I believe our lives are the same way. While this may admittedly be a personal bias (since I am also a musician), I believe music can intensify emotions and add significantly to a sense of well-being, joy, and happiness. It may even be the reason for the incredible popularity of *iTunes* and the *iPod*.

---

iTunes and *iPod*, are registered trademarks of Apple Computer

If music is not yet an integral part of your daily life, try it. It can enhance almost any situation. See if it works for you. It does for me. It certainly seems to create an "ambiance" that enhances my life and happiness every step along the way.

I use music while exercising, skiing, working, driving, flying, boating and of course, partying. Just about any situation can be positively enhanced with music. I even play music while I jog. It engages more of my senses as I marvel in wonder and appreciation at the beauty of the surroundings. It motivates me (and somewhat distracts me from the pain of running) so I can achieve a more productive workout. It also has a longer-term, more subtle benefit toward happiness. Many times, just hearing certain songs later brings back some of the great feelings I had while I was running in some beautiful places.

DO WHAT YOU LOVE

Chapter Two (*Identity, Purpose, and Passions*) describes how "loving what you do" may be just as fulfilling as "doing what you love." While this is true, it is certainly better to be able to derive your income from something you are passionate about. So while not a BeHappy! requirement, another tool for enhancing happiness is to chose a career involving something you love. If you are already in a career that doesn't qualify, you can either learn to love it as described in Chapter Two or make a change.

When I did that, it enhanced my life tremendously. I had wanted to be a doctor since as far back as I can remember. But after doing whatever it took to get into and through Medical School, which was very difficult (including many years of hard study) then living through the grueling experience of Residency, and finally starting a chain of emergency clinics, I unfortunately found I didn't love it and it didn't completely fit what I envisioned for my life, my identity, and my *Definition of Happiness.*

So I went back to school, got my MBA and got into business, first as the Medical Director of a small pharmaceutical company and working my way up to the CEO of a biotechnology company. I even took a major cut in pay to make this happen. But it was a great move and although I am still not truly *doing what I absolutely love*, I definitely *love what I do.*

It challenges me, helps fulfill my *Definition of Happiness*, represents growth, is consistent with my identity, and I am good at it. As an added benefit, this is where I met my soul mate — my wife, Jill. I never would have met her had I not made my career move. For that alone, it was well worth the effort, risk, and change.

So if you are not doing something you love — and especially if you really hate your job — this is another strategy to enhance the quality of your life and BeHappy!

USE YOUR TALENTS

Chapter Two touched on the relationship between your *purpose* and your talents. Surely, living consistent with your purpose in life — if you have one — will improve your ability to BeHappy! Additionally, by identifying or discovering what you are really good at — and using that gift in your life, you can be much happier and more fulfilled. Acknowledging and using your talents can also help you discover your *purpose*. By using your inherent talents, whether in your career or your personal life, you can increase your ability to BeHappy! tremendously. This should be part of your *Happiness Plan*.

You should have written some of your talents on page 28 in Chapter Two. Go back and see what you wrote and rewrite them in the spaces below. Add any you missed, or even fine-tune it down to one main talent of yours.

-
-
-

Did you write something down? If so, are you using this talent (or these talents) in your life? Is it part of your job or career? If you didn't write anything in the spaces above...why not? Have you not determined or discovered your talents? Do you have the false belief that you don't have any? The fact is, we all have some inherent gifts or talents. It's up to us to identify those gifts and use them. If we do, we will be happier. If we don't, we won't.

SET GOALS

Although not a primary focus of this book, it is important to have a basic understanding of your goals in life.[8] This was mentioned in Chapter Six, *Money and Happiness*. It is an important component of creating positive expectations for the future. Like answering the question — what is possible in your future? — defining your goals also creates possibility and positive expectations.

So, what are your top 5 goals in life? Write the answers to this question below — or in Appendix 3:

-
-
-
-
-

These top 5 goals should only be the start. There are many books, tapes, and other personal development materials describing various goal-setting processes. Use some of these to help regularly define and achieve the goals you have for your life. In many cases, this will augment your ability to BeHappy!.

CONSIDER RELIGION AND SPIRITUALITY

Many people derive great emotional benefit from religious belief and practice. People very close to me have told me that their religion — and the act of practicing that religion by going to church on Sunday's — helps to relieve the pain of personal loss, like the death of their parents.

In a more general sense, I have also heard it said that "religion is the prescription for an ailing soul." For some people this is surely true. For others, it is much more than that.

On a superficial level, religion can address many of the concepts described throughout this book. Practicing your religion can create and foster strong *relationships* and fulfill the concept of being part of a *team*. It can create a sense of *purpose* and *contribution* (most religious gatherings I have experienced allow you to contribute to them weekly). Religion can even create positive expectations for the future (discussed in Chapter Six) since surely the concept of heaven and eternal life is better than the alternative. Most times there's even *music* involved.

On a much deeper level, another quality of religion is the spiritual component. Spirituality, while a part of religion, is also a completely separate experience. Spirituality is the recognition of a higher consciousness and an appreciation for the vastness of our existence. A sunset, for example, can create a spiritual experience for me.

If religion is partly "a prescription for an ailing soul," then spirituality is "the preventative medicine." The religion part of the equation provides the structure and context for participating in that spirituality more formally and regularly.

You can augment your need for spirituality with a formal religious connection (like going to a church, synagogue, or similar place of worship) or you can just be very spiritual on your own, without the ties or need for a particular religion. Personally, I prefer the latter.

Again, as with much of this process to your own happiness, this is a personal matter, with no right or wrong answer. Whatever works for you. Your *Definition of Happiness* might even represent the role religion and/or spirituality plays in your life and your ability to BeHappy!

For some people, religion is an essential component of their *Definition*. For others, just being a spiritual person, without the "structure" involved in many religions is all that is necessary. For yet others, neither is essential for total happiness. We can be totally happy in any of these scenarios.

As I said, there is no right or wrong way. My good friend Naida uses a well-known phrase — "different strokes for different folks." Religion is surely a topic of "different strokes." So choose what's right for you to BeHappy!

DON'T WATCH THE NEWS

While this will not make me popular with the news media, my point is: to really be as happy as possible, we must focus more on the positives than the negatives of life. The news seems to focus almost exclusively on the negatives.

For years I have joked that they shouldn't call it the "News" at all, but rather what it really seems to be, which is "The **Bad** News." What benefits do we get, for example, by knowing that a woman and her two children were brutally murdered in Texas or that a private plane crashed in Colorado killing all seven people on board? Do we really need to know this? What greater purpose do they serve? These are the types of stories that make the headlines. It's what sells and improves the ratings.

To me, it provides little benefit — but it just seems bad news sells better than good news. People love to hear about the murders, suicides, rapes, accidents, crimes, terrorist attacks, and other negative events occurring in our world. It's sad, but good news is just not as exciting.

Because of this, long ago I stopped watching the news or even reading much of the newspaper and I must say, it has reduced anxiety and stress in my life and helped me focus on the positive things about our world. Bad news can put a negative veil over everything. I believe that focusing on the negatives is simply a bad strategy for happiness.

Please don't misunderstand; I definitely believe it is good to keep up with world and local events. So the challenge is to find a way to keep up with the important information you need while simultaneously avoiding the unnecessary negative "entertainment" involved in bad news. It can be done. Although I might miss a few things about what's happening in the world, if it's really important, I usually find out. And if the news is a source of entertainment for you, it can be achieved in many more positive ways. Just keep reading …

INCLUDE ENTERTAINMENT IN YOUR LIFE

Entertainment can enhance happiness greatly. And in our society, people seem to have realized this. Just look at the income levels of the people in the business of entertainment. Athletes, movie stars, writers, and musicians can make millions, even tens of millions per year. Why? Because there is high demand for these sources of entertainment, and anything in high demand will command a high price.

Just look at a typical Sunday in the United States during the months of September through January. More than 50,000 people in nearly every major city in the US pay up to $100 or more to go to a football game. The same is true of hockey, baseball, basketball, and even wrestling. People thrive on entertainment. And the reason is simple. With the complexities and stresses of everyday life, entertainment is a distraction at the very least.

But it is more than just distraction. We can learn a lot from some forms of entertainment. Movies, for example, are often not only entertaining but also educational, motivating and stimulating.

I've listed some of my favorite movies in the box to the right; especially ones providing a combination of learning, entertainment, and motivation.

> ## SOME GREAT MOVIES
>
> * It's a Wonderful Life
> * Forrest Gump
> * Braveheart
> * The Shawshank Redemption
> * The Cider House Rules
> * Good Will Hunting
> * Secondhand Lions
> * Kramer vs Kramer
> * Raiders of the Lost Arc
> * Legends of the Fall
> * Seabiscuit
> * Powder
> * Jersey Girl
> * Remember the Titans
> * The Kid

Some of them I consider educational and inspiring, like *Forrest Gump* and *The Shawshank Redemption*, while others are great mainly because of their entertainment value, like *Raiders of the Lost Arc* and *The Kid*.

Some others simply have a great message. I watch *It's A Wonderful Life* every year around the holidays. Not only is it entertaining, but also it is an annual reminder of how great life is and how much there is to appreciate about our relationships and our world. And George Bailey (the character Jimmy Stewart played in the movie) although never pursuing his passion, discovers that he is the happiest and "richest man in town"…all because of his relationships with his family and friends.

SPEND SOME TIME ALONE

Some people do not like to be alone. Others love it. Regardless of your preference, it can help to spend some time by yourself, preferably in a serene, beautiful place — and for more than a few minutes. If possible, several days is best.

There is so much beauty in the world. Taking some time to notice it can help in many ways. It can reduce stress and make you appreciate things more. The introspection can help solve problems. It can even become spiritual. And while it is great to share the beauty of the world with others, sometimes it is also great to appreciate it alone and just be with "yourself." It can be a time of reflection and self-awareness.

So on occasion, perhaps once a month, you might consider taking a few hours to actually be by yourself. This might involve waking up early on a beautiful Saturday morning and, instead of just rolling over, taking a walk alone at sunrise. Along the way, you might think about the things addressed in this book. Consider your goals and dreams. What contributions have you made lately? Are you living consistent with your identity? Are you using your talents? You might even want to amplify your experience by letting yourself be inspired by music while you walk.

Being alone for a few hours every week or so can help you focus and put life into perspective. Then, at least once a year, spend several days alone. Doing this will probably increase the gratitude you have for the things in your life right now. So, put together a strategy for ways to make this happen and what you might want to accomplish when you are alone and make a commitment to do it. You may discover that you cherish this time and it will become a special part of your life.

DON'T LET WHAT OTHERS THINK
RULE YOUR LIFE

Many people are so concerned about what others think of them, that they live their lives contrary to their true identity (remember the powerful affect identity has on happiness from Chapter Two). They try to look and act in ways meant to get approval from others, rather than being themselves to maximize their happiness.

For many people, this is not easy to avoid. Especially in our culture, where beauty is so valued, power so respected, and success so honored, we are constantly under pressure to be, or become, someone we're not.

Surely, maturity helps reduce this need. I know that I am much less concerned about what others think today than I was when I was 20 or 30. Still, it is something we should all learn to manage. If this is impacting your ability to be as happy as possible, there are many sources which can help. Another book in this series, **BeYou!**, will address this more thoroughly.

CONTRIBUTE TO OTHERS

Making a contribution to something or somebody on a regular basis is a great way to generate positive feelings and emotions. Big or small, doing something every month, every week, or possibly even every day will help make you happier.

It may sound overly simplistic, but there is nothing like the feeling of giving, of making a contribution to add meaning and fulfillment to life. If you have a clear *purpose* in life, and are fulfilling that *purpose*, you probably know the feeling since a *purpose* is generally associated with contribution.

If you are not in the habit of contributing regularly, you can begin by figuring out a way to make it happen often. You may even consider putting an alert in your planner and/or start writing down the contributions you have made on a daily, weekly and monthly basis. If you make it a habit, you will experience a noticeable, positive change in the way you feel.

To help you create your plan, list some ways you could contribute to someone or something on a regular basis here:

Daily

•

•

Weekly

•

•

Monthly

•

•

Yearly

•

•

Contribution will add tremendously to your sense of fulfillment, especially if you contributing on a regular basis. So go back over the lists you created for ways you can contribute. Are there more ways you can contribute? Big or small — it doesn't matter.

What is important is starting, because once you start and experience the positive feelings this elicits, it will become a regular part of your life. The box to the right provides some ideas to stimulate you on ways to contribute on a regular basis. You might use some of these, or any that work for you. The more ways you have to contribute, the more you will follow through with at least a few.

USE EMOTIONS

One important point to understand before you can be truly

EXAMPLES OF WAYS TO CONTRIBUTE:

Daily
• Help boost someone's self-confidence
• Give someone advice or counsel
• Send out an e-mail "thought for the day"
• Tell your spouse you love them
• Help someone solve a problem

Weekly
• Send a friend a note of gratitude
• Pay the toll for the car behind you
• Call an elderly person just to talk
• Buy someone a cup of coffee

Monthly
• Buy a meal for a homeless person
• Send an appreciation card to someone
• Take a friend or family member to dinner
• Take your pet to visit children with cancer
• Be a mentor to someone

Yearly
• Volunteer at a hospital
• Donate to a worthy cause
• Take food/gifts to a needy family
• Contribute to a child's education
• Create a "special day" for your children

happy is to think about how your *Definition of Happiness* relates to other pleasurable emotions in your life.

For example, you can be having great fun in your life, experiencing many positive emotions on a regular basis, but still be unhappy overall because you are stressed or unfulfilled. As addressed earlier, it is most likely this may well be a consequence of not having fulfilled your *Definition of Happiness*.

Understanding this concept clearly is important since the process of becoming happy can be helped or hindered with positive and negative emotions. Our overall goal is to experience as many of the positive emotions and as few of the negative emotions as possible.

On the negative side, for example, *fear* and *guilt* are two emotions which carry the most impact in terms of preventing happiness. In the film the *Shawshank Redemption*, Red (the character Morgan Freeman portrayed in the movie) who has been in prison for 40 years stated, *"fear is the worst thing a man can experience."*

And surely, undue fear is a terrible emotion, which could derail your happiness (remember my Living In Fear Everyday acronym for LIFE at the beginning of the book). So, it is important for you to avoid undue fear in your life — but how? Well, there are many tools discussed in this book which can help you achieve that objective, as well as help to avoid other negative emotions.

For example, as I stressed in the chapter on money, struggling with a significant debt load can create a constant source of fear, regardless of your risk tolerance. If your debt becomes too significant, you may fear losing everything, sense a fear of failure, and even begin to fear health problems related to stress. So just by staying out of debt as described in Chapter Six, you can reduce some fear in your life.

Making a commitment to a solid, monogamous relationship not only creates a context for intimacy, it can also decrease the fear of contracting a possible deadly sexually transmitted disease — a reality of life these days. And it helps you avoid the inevitable guilt associated with violating your integrity and honesty.

The point here is not to preach about morality, but rather provide some examples of emotions that can jeopardize happiness. It is up to each of us to do whatever it takes to help improve the quality of our lives.

To increase the positive emotions in your life, here is some additional information to consider as you create your *Happiness Plan* in the next chapter:

Examples of Positive Emotions which can help you BeHappy!

Contentment: A general sense of well being which involves appreciating what you have as you enjoy the process of life.

Peace-of-Mind: Requires you to live your life in harmony with your identity and expectations. Being yourself, having true companionship and maintaining minimal debt are great ways to enjoy this emotion.

Wealth: This not only refers to the tangible financial resources usually associated with the word, but also the great *feeling* associated with how you lead a "rich" life. (People can feel wealthy, emotionally, even if they do not have much money).

Fun: To really have fun, you must know what it is you love to do most. What is really exciting or stimulating to you? Once you know this, make sure to take action. *Just Do It.* Fun is generally an "acute" or short-term emotion, so it doesn't hurt to experience it as frequently as possible.

One element used to distinguish happiness from many other emotions or feelings is a "time factor". We are defining *happiness* as a long-term feeling or phenomenon, which, once established, lasts years, decades and ideally, your entire life. All the other sensations are generally short-term, temporary emotions.

You can be having fun for an hour, a day, a week, a month or even a year, for example, but in general, it is not what you do or experience during any brief period of time that creates long-term happiness. Happiness is more of a constant *state of mind* than a temporary emotional feeling.

In other words, it is a mentality — an attitude — which cuts through negative times, allowing you to get through tough periods more easily and possibly even appreciate the challenge of the struggle. In fact, you can be under considerable stress, with things going wrong all around you, and still BeHappy! I'm sure you can think of a time like that in your life. This was discussed thoroughly in Chapter Eight, *Dealing With the Tough Times*.

Without wanting to be too cute about it, perhaps it's somewhat like the difference between *love* and *lust*. Sometimes they may feel so similar that you can't even tell which is which. Over the long-term, however, each of these emotions can lead you to an entirely different result. *Lust* is generally associated with a temporary feeling, while love is a deeper feeling that can last forever. Also, continuing with the analogy, just as lust can lead to love, so too can fun or enjoyment lead to happiness. And, like with all the emotions related to happiness, if you can maintain *lust* along with *love* in your relationship, so much the better (just like maintaining fun and excitement in your journey to happiness).

NEGATIVE EMOTIONS TO AVOID IN YOUR LIFE

Negative emotions can be both good and bad. As discussed in Chapter Eight, *Dealing With the Tough Times*, life's challenges can also be great learning events, character-building opportunities and significant growth experiences.

On the other hand, there are many useless, unproductive negative emotions that should be avoided. The fewer of these you experience on a daily basis, the more opportunity you will have to appreciate life, nurture relationships and make progress toward your goals. So, taking steps to minimize some of the more common negative emotions can be helpful. Here are a few to avoid:

Hate: Hate is an emotion you should consider eliminating completely from your life — and even from your vocabulary. Nothing productive comes from hate. You can dislike things, but to hate is a useless, negative investment in a person, place or thing obviously unworthy of all that attention, especially when it comes to other human beings or cultures. Remember the concept of embracing and appreciating diversity from Chapter Seven (rules).

Worry: The important thing to remember about this emotion is that, ultimately, it doesn't serve any real purpose. Worry cannot change an outcome, except perhaps to increase the possibility of a negative outcome happening which might not otherwise have occurred.[9] So take steps to reduce worry from your life. As they say, "don't sweat the small stuff … and it is all small stuff" or another favorite … "*don't worry — be happy.*"

> "*Worry never robs tomorrow of its sorrow; it just saps the joy out of today*"
>
> — *Leo Buscaglia*

Jealousy: There will always be people better off and worse off than you. Jealousy is another emotion that, at the end of the day, serves very little purpose except to upset you. I acknowledge the possibility that being a bit envious of someone could motivate you to do better in your life, but there are better ways to motivate yourself.

Anxiety: As with worry, anxiety changes nothing. While it can create a "call to action", it can also reduce your effectiveness and affect relationships.

Guilt: Guilt, which can be associated with *regret*, is an emotion you should avoid. Since it is related to regret, the strategies in Chapter Nine on *regrets* are important tools to help you minimize feelings of guilt.

Have you noticed there are some commonly experienced emotions missing from this list you might consider negative? One of these is *frustration*. While frustration can be painful, it can also be quite motivating and productive. So while you do not want to live life in a frustrated state, it is probably an emotion that can help you along on your journey to BeHappy! and achieve your life's goals.

So, as you create your personal *Happiness Plan* in the next chapter, consider the emotions you experience on a daily basis. Which are positive, productive emotions and which are negative, unproductive ones? Do you experience more negative emotions than positive ones? Make sure to include in your *Plan* ways to increase the positive emotions in your life and decrease the negative ones, remembering that some negative emotions are a fact of life and can even be helpful.

> *"In our fanaticism to accomplish great things and accumulate wealth, we are forgetting the art of living simply."*
>
> — From **"Simple Living in a Complex World"** by David Irvine

SIMPLIFY YOUR LIFE

Most would agree that life can be complex — especially today, where the pace of our world is intense and continues to increase dramatically. We are always "connected," have constant pressure and responsibilities, and are surrounded by so much opportunity that it can be difficult to "slow down."

David Irvine's book, *Simple Living in a Complex World* provides a wonderful process for simplifying life in today's hectic and achievement-oriented culture. And it doesn't mean we must achieve less or reduce our desire to accumulate wealth.

In his book, for example, David relays something he heard from Mahatma Gandhi when asked how he was able to accomplish so much in his lifetime. Gandhi replied, *"The way that I am able to accomplish so much is that I mediate two hours a day, unless I am very busy, then I mediate four hours a day."*

This means getting down to basics. Many of these basics are what are described throughout this book.

Setting priorities, living in the present, staying out of debt, being able to appreciate what you have and nurturing relationship are all part of it.

These strategies, and others — like those found in Irvine's book, which I recommend highly — can help you simplify your life, achieve more, and **BeHappy!**

CHAPTER SUMMARY & KEY POINTS

1. There are many "little things" you can do to add positive influences to your daily life. Many involve personal preference and are different for everyone.

2. To be really happy, it is important to include as many things as possible in your life that make things more pleasant.

3. Various emotions, both positive and negative, can be used (or avoided) to help create better, more lasting happiness.

4. In general, it is good to include as many positive emotions in your life and exclude as many negative emotions to help you be happier.

5. By simplifying your life, you can achieve many things simultaneously, like living in the moment, enjoying the process, and increasing peace-of-mind.

11

CREATING YOUR PERSONAL "HAPPINESS PLAN"

THE BeHappy! "SYSTEM"

The key to all this BeHappy! stuff is that no one exercise — no one tool — will create total happiness by itself. It is a commitment to the process, followed by a system of actions, activities, and events that will do it; nothing more and nothing less.

> "Most folks are as happy as they make up their minds to be."
>
> — Abraham Lincoln

MONITORING AND DOCUMENTING YOUR PROGRESS

Like any journey, it is critical to know where we are throughout the trip to allow for any necessary adjustments. To best achieve this, we must monitor how we are doing on a regular basis.

Part of the monitoring process involves realizing what is making us happy at many points along the way and relishing that happiness. Just realizing all the great things about our existence, and being grateful for life, is part of being completely happy.

Many people are actually happier than they think. They have much more for which to be grateful than they realize. Life is challenging and stressful, and there are many tough times. As you have learned with this book — if you have completed the exercises and are using the tools — happiness can exist regardless of the challenges, setbacks, and difficulties we experience in our lives. You probably know people who are under high stress or have had major hardships and yet they are very happy. Also, you may know someone who has an "easy" life, but is still unhappy and unfulfilled.

There are many reasons for this phenomenon. The most common is a lack of gratitude for what they already have, and many times all it takes is a focused and conscious effort to step back, realize how great things really are, and just appreciate life; even for just a few minutes. Documenting your activities — like with pictures — and monitoring your progress will help.

Some may be thinking right now, "that's easier said than done". And, you are right. It isn't easy. It's certainly much easier to focus on what's wrong with our lives and what we don't have. What makes it much easier, however, is to (a) know what makes (or will make) you happy, (b) document and monitor your progress, and (c) notice the beauty of life.

> *"It's the people who can sit and enjoy a sunset that are the happiest."*
>
> *— **Woody Harrelson**
> in the movie,
> **After The Sunset***

A beautiful sunset.

I keep a running "tally" of things in my life that are fun, exciting, fulfilling, memorable, etc. Every year, throughout the year, I create my "Year in Review" list. I have it in my PDA-cell phone. It is with me always (it even has a camera built in so I can take pictures of spontaneous great moments). I update it every week or two and look back at it at least once a month. And, amazingly, every time I review it, I get the same sense of appreciation, happiness and fulfillment

I got when I was actually in the moment. It's truly amazing how it works. Keeping a journal is another great way of achieving this and is a great habit to form.

> *"If happiness is just around the corner, turn often"*

It's really somewhat like a "real-time" version of the process completed in Chapter Three where we listed everything that made us happy over the past week, month, year, decade, etc. Only with this tool, we are writing it down as we go through life — every week — and reviewing it regularly. It works extremely well.

Start doing this, along with the rest of the exercises and tools in this book, and gradually you will become happier and more fulfilled in your life. It's like a constant reminder of how great life is. And, it also helps to remind us of what things we want more frequent in our lives. Pictures add a visual component to this process.

THE SYSTEM...

As you may realize by now, to BeHappy! you need to be proactive. It does not always just happen. The fact that you've bought and read this book is proof. And if you've gone through the exercises seriously, and started to use the tools described throughout the book, you probably notice that there is a "system" to it all.

To capture some of the important points in the system on becoming as happy as you can in life, here are the 10 key components:

1. Make sure you know what happiness means for you.
   Update your *Definition of Happiness* regularly and review it frequently. Make sure you have the checklist of the components of this definition handy (see pages 6 and 12). And, if you didn't do the exercise in Chapter One — do it.

2. Know who you are and live in sync with that identity.
   Chapter Two provides a start to achieving this objective. If this is a significant issue in your life, though, there are many sources to help you with this.

3. Explore your purpose in life, your passions, and your talents. Use these tools (again in Chapter Two) to move closer to a life of fulfillment, fun, and freedom.

4. Create, manage, and maintain great relationships in your life. This is the single most crucial component of happiness. Review Chapter Four if necessary.

5. Know what has made you happy in the past (even temporarily). This involves anything that made you feel good; anything pleasurable, fun, fulfilling, gratifying, growth-oriented or impactful. Review Chapter Three and keep making lists as you think of things that make you happy.

6. Create better health through happiness, gratitude, and a healthy lifestyle. As a result, your happiness will be further enhanced. Chapter Five addresses this part of the system.

7. Manage your expectations and stay out of unreasonable debt. Money — like it or not — is part of the system. Chapter Six describes how.

8. Reduce the number of rules that dictate the way you live and feel. Chapter Eight describes how

9. Minimize the potential to develop significant regrets in your life. The methods described in Chapter Nine can help.

10. Use whatever "tool" work best for you in keeping the system moving in the positive direction. Some of those tools (from Chapter Ten) are:

   • Take pictures of the things you do — especially the fun, pleasurable, exciting parts of your daily life. The more the better. This will create a visual reminder for you of what is important and pleasurable to you.

   • Review your lists and pictures at least every 3 months. Put the best pictures of great moments up and around your work and home; wherever you spend time (including pictures of some of your goals for incentive and motivation).

The screensaver on your computers are great places to have continuous exposure to your happiness.

- Never stop improving.

- Be part of a team. Join one or start one.

- Appreciate what you have in your life right now.

- Use music as your life's "soundtrack."

- Create a process of writing down everything you do that creates pleasure and gratitude in your life. You must commit to this process and do it weekly, monthly, and yearly.

- Contribute to something or someone regularly. Find new, creative ways to contribute.

- Have goals and reward yourself when you achieve them.

What all this implies is: don't wait for some event, financial goal, or life achievement to be happy. BeHappy! NOW!

You have gone this far, now complete the system by having a plan to make it real, reliable, an reviewable.

CREATING YOUR PERSONAL "HAPPINESS PLAN"...

Creating an action plan to happiness now "simply" involves organizing the information you generated in this book, using the tools you found most useful, and building a useable process to achieve the happiness you want. I call it your *Happiness Plan*.

Ideally, this *Happiness Plan* you create can be kept with you somewhere where you can access it regularly. I keep mine in my PDA (Personal

> *"Happy are those who dream dreams and are ready to pay the price to make them come true."*
>
> **— Leon J. Suenens**

Digital Assistant), which is also a cell phone and camera, so I can refer to it wherever I am, whenever I want.

The blueprint of your Personal *Happiness Plan* is found after the Postscript, in Appendix 1. Take the time to fill it in completely. Refer to the exercises you completed throughout this journey as a guide.

You can copy this plan — either in hard copy or into your PDA. This is your "map".[10] Use it! You will see how happiness increases throughout your life's journey.

POSTSCRIPT

LTHOUGH I KNEW when I finished writing this book that it would contain many fundamental concepts and tools to make people happier, I still felt something was missing. In fact, there is much more to say on the topic of happiness and I am sure you agree. While I hope this book goes a long way to help you **BeHappy!** there is certainly so much to happiness and all human emotion, that it cannot be resolved fully in a book this brief.

That is why I created and am in process of writing the entire **BeHappy!** series. This volume is the first in what is intended to be a comprehensive program designed to enhance the quality of your life in all areas. That's why I would like your feedback, comments, and experiences. Through my website, *www.behappy101.com*, you can provide your remarks on the progress you have made and the challenges you experience in your journey. I would also like to know how to continually improve the results this book provides. Your thoughts and suggestions will be appreciated.

The goal of this new **BeHappy!** series is to address everything necessary to have the most incredible life possible: full of happiness, fulfillment, wealth, fun, health, and peace-of-mind. But as we all know, everyone's definition of a "great life" is different. For some, a great life may be the pursuit of *purpose*, with no priority placed on wealth or material possessions. For someone else, money and business success are critical for a "great life." Neither is right or wrong and everything is possible. It's just another thing that's great about life…we are all different.

Regardless of your requirements for a great life, few of us would disagree that happiness is one common denominator we all seek.[11] I hope, therefore, that this book will be viewed as a starting point for your journey to an incredible life of happiness, gratitude and fulfillment. However, to truly realize your goal of ultimate happiness, it may really only be possible when you master all the elements in the **BeHappy!** series that relate to you personally.

Yes…you can have an awesome life without following all the strategies and tools in the series. But for the best life possible, it's really a comprehensive, continuous process of small improvements that will get you there.

Since topics of the BeHappy! series are so broad, let me suggest which ones you will find to be most closely associated with happiness for most people. In other words, if you can read only five more books in the series, the ones that could be most helpful are:

- BeTogether!
- BeHealthy!
- BeBalanced!
- BeFulfilled!
- BeWealthy!

These five books, plus this one, BeHappy! should give you a great foundation for a happy life in today's complex world.

Getting deeper into the crucial role *relationships* play in life is the subject of BeTogether!, which will be an exploration of how to build and retain strong relationships with a loving spouse, significant other, your children, your friends, and your business colleagues. Again, this is the biggest component of happiness for most people.

As mentioned earlier, being healthy is also an important component of *happiness*. You may not realize this until you lose it or if you already have health problems. Being proactive is the key, and so BeHealthy! will help guide you to become more proactive so that you can either avoid future health issues or better deal with the ones you are experiencing.

Being *balanced* involves defining, reorganizing, and managing the major priorities in your life. Striving for balance in your life can build upon a foundation that will take you to a whole new level of personal joy. This is the focus of BeBalanced!, which intends to help achieve these objectives in a simple, easy-to-follow format.

Being *fulfilled* can occur regardless of your success at finding financial abundance and balance. In BeFulfilled!, another completely independent aspect of happiness is explored. For example, some people with little money and/or balance in their lives can still be fulfilled. BeFulfilled! will show you how.

Wealth, while not a priority for everyone, can be a major factor for many people in improving quality of life. **BeWealthy!** will provide various tools to help you achieve your financial goals or needs. The tools in **BeWealthy!** can help you at least build a stable financial foundation and perhaps even help you achieve financial abundance.

> *"Those who wish to sing always find a song."*
>
> —*Swedish Proverb*

A FINAL THOUGHT: One of my objectives for this book — and for the entire **BeHappy!** series — is to make achieving the result very simple. That is not always easy. For happiness, to boil it down to the absolute simplest possible concept, just remember "THE THREE R's" ... Relationships, Rules, and Regrets. If you take away nothing more from this book, to improve happiness significantly, just:

1. Focus on creating and maintaining some great RELATION-SHIPS, especially with a soul-mate and with your children;

2. Reduce or eliminate the RULES that guide your life and understand as many of the RULES as possible of those people closest to you;

3. Minimize the potential for REGRETS in your life, and as much as possible, take the necessary steps to deal with the REGRETS you may already have.

Do these three things, and you can **BeHappy!**

—*Jimmy DeMesa, M.D.*

APPENDIX 1
PERSONAL
"HAPPINESS PLAN"

Name:

Date:

Home address:

Current job:

My personal *Definition of Happiness* is:

The major things required in my life to make me happy, therefore, are:

❑

❑

❑

❑

❑

These are the things I must make sure I work on everyday to ensure they are in my life.

The things currently missing in my life from the checklist above are:

-

-

-

-

For each of the items in the list above of things currently missing from my life that are required to fulfill my *Definition of Happiness*, the actions I will take to make certain they are present in my life are:

Item #1:
Actions:
This week:
This month:
This year:
This decade:

Item #2:
Actions:
This week
This month:
This year:
This decade:

Item #3:
Actions:
This week:
This month:
This year:
This decade:

Item #4:
Actions:
This week:
This month:
This year:
This decade:

The roles I currently play in my life are:

The main roles I want to play in my life include:

My main passions in life are:

My plan to include more of these passions in my life is as follows:

Other things I will include in my life on a regular basis are:

Examples include music, time alone, a pet, exercise, maintaining an ideal body weight, taking a friend to lunch, spending more time with family, taking pictures, keeping a journal, entertainment, etc.

The most important relationships in my life are:

-
-
-
-

The things I will do to nurture these relationships include:

-
-
-
-

My purpose in life is:

To fulfill that purpose in life, I must:

-
-
-
-

My current top 5 goals are:

1.

2.

3.

4.

5.

My general strategies to achieve those goals are:

Goal 1.

Goal 2.

Goal 3.

Goal 4.

Goal 5.

My rules (or guidelines) in life are:

•

•

•

•

The rules of my most significant personal relationship(s) are:

•

•

•

•

Things I must do to make sure our rules conflict as little as possible:

•

•

•

•

Things I will make sure to never (or never again) regret doing in my life:

•

•

•

•

Things I will make sure to never regret NOT doing in my life:

-
-
-
-

The positive emotions I want in my life daily are:

-
-
-
-

Ways to make sure each of these emotions exists in my life are:

Emotion	Ways to include this emotion in my life
•	•
•	•
•	•
•	•

The negative emotions I want to minimize in my life are:

-
-
-
-

Ways to make sure each of these emotions is minimized in my life are:

Emotion	Ways to exclude this emotion from my life
•	•
•	•
•	•
•	•

Some of the "tough times" I have had in my life are:

-
-
-
-

The way I will deal with similar "tough times" if they occur again are:

-
-
-
-

Some of the "tough times" that could occur in the future are:

-
-
-
-

The way I will prepare for these "tough times" if they occur are:

-
-
-
-

Contributions I will make on a daily, weekly, monthly, and yearly basis are:

-
-
-
-

Things I will do to simplify my life are:

•

•

•

•

•

•

•

•

Other things I will do to BeHappy!

•

•

•

•

•

•

•

•

APPENDIX 2
"YEAR IN REVIEW"
WORKSHEET

THIS BOOK MENTIONS THAT DOCUMENTING THE POSITIVES IN YOUR LIFE IS A GREAT TOOL BY WHICH TO INCREASE YOUR HAPPINESS. ONE WAY TO DO THIS REGULARLY IS TO CREATE A "YEAR IN REVIEW" PROCESS WHICH YOU FILL IN AS YOU GO THROUGH EVERY YEAR, THEN REVIEW REGULARLY TO "RECREATE" THE POSITIVE FEELINGS AND EMOTIONS THESE "MOMENTS" GENERATED. HERE IS A BLUEPRINT FOR THAT PROCESS. YOU SHOULD REVISE IT TO FIT YOUR LIFE (IN OTHER WORDS, TO HELP YOU FOCUS ON THE KINDS OF THINGS FROM CHAPTER 3 THAT MAKE YOU HAPPY).

YEAR: _____

Memorable activities, events, and circumstances:

-
-
-
-
-
-
-
-
-
-

Movies watched:

-
-
-
-
-
-

Books read:

-
-
-
-
-
-

Major accomplishments:

-
-
-
-
-
-

Relationships created or nurtured:

-
-
-
-
-
-

APPENDIX 3
EXERCISES FROM BeHappy!

USE THESE PAGES ONLY IF YOU PREFER NOT TO WRITE YOUR ANSWERS IN THE SPACES PROVIDED WITHIN EACH CHAPTER AND WANT TO TEAR THESE PAGES OUT. IT IS EASIER AND MORE PRODUCTIVE, HOWEVER, TO DO THE EXERCISES DIRECTLY WITHIN EACH CHAPTER.

PART ONE: THE FOUNDATION
CHAPTER ONE: *Your Definition of Happiness*

Definition of Happiness (from page 6)

The Main criteria of your *Definition of Happiness (from page 12)*

-
-
-
-
-

CHAPTER TWO: *Identity, Purpose, and Passions*

Your Purpose in life (from page 17):

The 3 to 5 things that are most important to you in life (from page 25):

•

•

•

•

•

The Top 5 ROLES you play in your life (from page 26):

•

•

•

•

•

The Top 5 standards you live your life by (from page 27):

Be

Be

Be

Be

Be

What do you love to do? (from page 27)

•

•

What are your talents? (from page 28)

•

•

Re-write your pupose in life here:

CHAPTER THREE: *What Makes You Happy?*

What are the most important things missing from your life? (from page 32)

•

•

•

•

•

What could you add to your life to make you happier? (from page 33)

•

•

•

•

•

Positive activities, events, achievements from the past WEEK (from pages 34–35)

Monday:

Tuesday:

Wednesday:

Thursday:

Friday:

Saturday:

Sunday:

The common themes from the above are:

•

•

•

•

Positive activities, events, achievements from the past MONTH (from page 37)

•

•

•

•

•

The common themes from the above are:

•

•

•

•

Positive activities, events, achievements from the past YEAR (from page 40)

-

-

-

-

Positive activities, events, achievements from the past DECADE (from page 43)

-

-

-

-

Positive activities, events, achievements from YOUR CHILDHOOD (from page 46)

-

-

-

-

-

What has made you unhappy in your life? (from page 47)

-

-

-

-

What could make you happier in the next 5 YEARS? (from page 49)

-

-

-

What could make you happier in the next 20 YEARS? (from page 49)

-
-
-
-

What are the common themes from the previous 8 exercises? (from page 50)

-
-
-
-

Re-write your *Definition of Happiness* (from page 51):

The 3major things that have made you unhappy in the past? (from page 51)

-
-
-

The 5 most important things that have made you happy in the past? (from page 51)

-
-
-

PART TWO: ESSENTIAL ELEMENTS

CHAPTER FOUR:
Relationships: The Ultimate "Happiness Loop"

List the people whose relationships are most important to you. Use the spaces below and place each person's name in the appropriate category (from page 61):

Immediate Family	Extended Family	Friends	Business and other
•	•	•	•
•	•	•	•
•	•	•	•
•	•	•	•
•	•	•	•

Ways to nurture and support the most important relationships:

•

•

•

•

•

•

•

List of 10 ways to make a special person feel special regularly (from pages 62–63):

1.

2.

3.

4.

5.

6.

7.

8.

9.

10.

CHAPTER 6:
Money and Happiness

What is possible in your future? (from page 79)

-
-
-
-
-
-

Things you can appreciate right now in your life (from page 83):

-
-
-
-
-
-

CHAPTER 7:
Changing Your Rules

The rules you have created for how you live your life are (from page 91):

•

•

•

•

•

Your rules changed to guidelines (from page 92):

RULE   GUIDELINE

•

•

•

•

Your reduced list of rules (from page 93):

•

•

•

The rules of your closest relationship in life are (from page 93):

•

•

•

•

•

CHAPTER 9:
Regrets

What have you done already (as of today) you regret doing? (from page 114):

•

•

•

•

What have you NOT DONE yet, but could be capable of doing at some point in your life that you would regret doing? (from page 116):

•

•

•

•

What have you NOT DONE yet that you might regret NOT HAVING DONE in your life? (from page 117):

•

•

•

•

Action plan to reduce/eliminate regrets (from page 119):

REGRET   ACTION

•

•

•

•

PART FOUR:
CREATING YOUR PERSONAL HAPPINESS PLAN

CHAPTER TEN: *Some Extra Tools*

Re-write your talents (from page 131):

•

•

•

Your top 5 goals in life (from page 132):

•

•

•

•

•

Ways you can contribute regularly (from pages 137–138):

Daily

•

•

Weekly

•

•

Monthly

•

•

Yearly

•

•

NOTES

CHAPTER ONE

[1] Beginning with the end in mind is a concept identified by many personal development experts. The book, *The 7 Habits of Highly Effective People*, by Stephen R. Covey describes it well.

[2] IMPORTANT ADVICE: Some people get stuck here and can't move on because they really can't figure out what makes them happy. If this happens — AND ONLY IF THIS HAPPENS — you can skip to Chapter Three, complete the exercises found there, then come back to Chapter One and Two. It is better, however, to get something down here for your *Definition of Happiness*, and then come back to it later once you have a better understanding of what can make you happy.

[3] Lance Armstrong was diagnosed with testicular cancer at the age of twenty-three, going through the debilitating process of chemotherapy and recovery before winning his first *Tour de France* in 1998. Since his experience, he has become an inspiration to cancer victims worldwide.

CHAPTER TWO

[4] This relative relationship between these three fundamental characteristics is based my own research, observations and opinions. There is no scientific study, which determined this relationship.

CHAPTER FIVE

[5] For a great perspective on how the mind affects the body, health, and longevity, read the book by Deepak Chopra, *Ageless Body, Timeless Mind*.

CHAPTER SIX

[6] There are many financial books and courses available to help create a wealth-building plan. Choose the one most suitable to you and follow it.

CHAPTER EIGHT

7 You can find out more about this great story at:
http://thelink.concordia.ca/article.pl?sid=03/03/04/0525209.
http://www.reachdisability.org/dsa/sailing_saved_mylife.shtml
http://www.camagazine.com/multimedia/camagazine/Library/FR/1996/Apr//ne
wsf.pdf

CHAPTER TEN

8 Anthony Robbins has a great "Goals Setting" process described in his best-selling book, *Awaken The Giant Within* and in several of his seminars and programs.

9 This concept involves a phenomenon described in many personal development books which relates to "getting what you focus on". If you focus on something negative (i.e., worry) you may just get it. Also, worry can make us less efficient and less creative in finding solutions to problems.

CHAPTER ELEVEN

10 In this context, map refers to two things. First, as described at the beginning of the book, this process is a journey. *Your Happiness Plan* can be used as a "roadmap" on that journey. I also use the term "map" to refer to a Massive Action Plan. Sometimes it takes "massive action" to achieve a goal or desired result.

POSTSCRIPT

11 It is certainly possible that there may be some people who have a desire to be unhappy. This is generally a psychological issue beyond the scope of this book (and the entire BeHappy! series). The assumption made here is that, if you are reading this book, like the majority of people you desire happiness as part of your "great life."

THE 10 BOOKS IN
THE BeHappy! Series

BeHappy!

Coming to the Series:

BeWealthy!

BeTogether!

BeBalanced!

BeYou!

BeHealthy!

BeFulfilled!

BeSuccessful!

BeOrganized!

BeComplete!

for more information go to:

www.behappy101.com

If you found this book thought provoking…
If you are interested in having this author…
or another of our consulting authors
design a workshop or seminar for your
company, organization, school, or team…

Let the experienced and knowledgeable group of experts
at *The Diogenes Consortium* go to work for you.
With literally hundreds of years of combined experience in:

Ethics • Human Resources • Employee Retention
Management • Pro-Active Leadership • Teams
Encouragement • Empowerment • Motivation
Attitute Modification • Energizing • Delegating Responsibility
Spirituality in the Workplace
Presentations to start-ups and Fortune 500 companies,
tax-exempt organizations and schools of all sizes
(public & private, elementary through university)

Call today for a list of our
authors/speakers/presenters/consultants
Call toll free at 866-602-1476
Or visit:
www.FocusOnEthics.com